Rewild

*Stories and Inspiration for
the Modern Adventurer*

Doron & Stephanie Francis

Rewild

*Stories and Inspiration for
the Modern Adventurer*

Hardie Grant

TRAVEL

Contents

Why we go

....

You may have felt it before. A surge of joy, a feeling of wholeness, a spontaneous connection to something greater than yourself. Those moments when the sun sets or rises, sitting quietly by a mountain or the sea. There might be a shiver down your spine, an emotional shift – a kind of release. It's perfectly normal, this feeling. It's called experiencing nature. That connection is a sense of belonging in the natural world.

For many, that feeling seems like it's slipping ever further out of our grasp. For the first time in history, more people live in urban areas than not. As our opportunities to experience nature grow narrower, it seems no coincidence that stress, obesity, anxiety, attention disorders and depression are on the rise. There is even a name for it: Nature Deficit Disorder, summed up by the range of behavioural issues that arise when human beings, especially children, don't spend enough of their time outside.

Technology isn't helping matters. It has become embedded in our lives, and with it the so-called 'attention economy' works hard to vie for our time and attention. Some studies suggest that, on average, we check our devices a mind-boggling 85 times a day. Paradoxically, the connectivity our phones and computers seem to promise us has left us feeling less plugged in to each other.

That said there has been a broad shift in attitude, particularly amongst the young who see digital detoxing as a natural and necessary reaction to our over-mediated, over-curated lives.

Science is catching up to what we intuitively know: that time spent in nature – the more, the better – has a positive effect on our wellbeing. It decreases stress, lowers heart rate and blood pressure, increases creativity and promotes clearer thought. Enter the modern phenomena of therapeutic camping programs; forest preschools for kids; tech-free retreats; city planners putting 'green' space at the heart of their designs and doctors prescribing their patients a walk in the park.

The journey that led us to creating our store and blog Homecamp, plus our books *Homecamp*, *Tent Life* and now *Rewild*, came from our own experiences retreating from our plugged-in lives and rediscovering the simple joys of being outdoors.

Over the years, we have been lucky enough to go on some epic adventures. We hiked in South-East Asia and the Andes;

explored the depths of the Amazonian jungle; watched bears in one of Russia's most remote corners; and travelled around our native Australia and New Zealand. But it was a camping road trip to California's High Sierra and coastal Big Sur that inspired us to create Homecamp. Somewhere in the grand meadows, amongst the giant sequoia trees, we fell in love with the idea of starting a brand centred around the idea of inspiring people to get outside, exploring our world's many beautiful places without leaving a negative imprint behind. We were frustrated with the modern concept of buying products that would break within a couple of uses only to be replaced without question, creating endless waste for landfill. When we camped, we wanted useful, well-designed products that would last us a lifetime.

Rewild is not about aspiring to travel to far-flung places, becoming an elite outdoorsperson or conquering the wild. It's about celebrating a simple truth: you don't need to be *doing* anything to connect with nature. It's about how just *being* in nature is enough.

This book is about adventurous everyday people – photographers, architects, chefs, writers, builders, seekers, thinkers, risk-takers – who are reuniting with nature in diverse ways, and with transformative results. Their stories all start with a desire to connect with the world around them, to step out of the daily grind and find a different, wilder, less trodden path. Their stories prove that getting back to nature isn't as hard as you might think.

From alternative ways of living – in a van, or a shipping container, or simply out of a backpack – to being alone in the woods, biking across continents, gazing at stars and surfing through frigid waves, these stories are all about inspiring you to spend more time outdoors. Maybe you've been meaning to take that camping trip with friends, or maybe you've been dreaming of a life on the road. Perhaps you are looking for inspiration on how to

start your own outdoor movement. In these pages, we think you'll find the push you need.

For us, camping is a fun and easy gateway to nature. Almost anyone can camp. It's inexpensive, and a realm in which learning a few simple skills opens up a broad range of adventures. Finding and chopping wood, making a fire and cooking a meal on its hot coals are activities almost as ancient as humanity itself, and hugely satisfying. Our how-to guide will get you started on developing these simple skills and planning your own adventures, whether they be in your backyard or off in the bush.

Rewild is all about finding new ways to switch off, create meaningful experiences and a heightened connection to the Earth. As contributor Graham Hiemstra says, nature is not a trend or a fad, it's something we need – this is something we humbly hope to inspire.

..........x

Doron & Stephanie, founders of Homecamp

Homecamp is an outdoor lifestyle brand that aims to inspire people to get outside and experience nature as much as possible. Launched in 2014, Homecamp has built up a loyal legion of followers and customers who want to enjoy the outdoors equipped with products and skills that will last a lifetime. www.homecamp.com.au

"

Rewild is all about finding new ways to switch off; to create meaningful experiences and a heightened connection to the earth.

How-to guide

Some practical advice for
fellow nature-lovers.

HOW TO PLAN FOR A CAR CAMPING TRIP

One of the many joys of camping with transport, whether that's a four-wheel-drive setup, camper van or just a car, is that it lets you set up a fully functional and comfortable campsite. Lightweight camping is great, but there's nothing like a camp out in nature with a few home comforts to make it that much more enjoyable. It encourages you to stay awhile and tune in to your surroundings. It allows you to take along items you would never consider on a lightweight adventure: a large tent, a comfortable mattress, a cool box, a camp kitchen, cast-iron cooking gear – maybe even a camp shower. Let these tips guide you to car camping greatness.

Research destinations and routes before you leave. The internet can be a fount of great information, but local knowledge and in-the-know friends are the best resources for finding 'The Spot'.

Check to see what sort of road leads in to the campsite and if your car can handle the conditions. Make sure to check whether you can drive your car up to the campsite too – otherwise you'll have to carry your gear in.

Check conditions: you'll want to be prepared for both the weather and the environment you will be camping in. Arrive well before sundown – the earlier the better, to avoid setting up camp in the dark.

Create a checklist of the essentials and non-essentials you want to take (see opposite page).

Get to know your gear before heading off. Set up your tent at least once before departing. Note the best way to pack and unpack it, and ensure all poles and pegs are safely stowed. Don't forget to pack your mallet!

Plan your meals and, if possible, prep as much food as possible beforehand. Pack food into resealable plastic bags or portable containers – even better, use a vacuum sealer (a worthwhile investment). Pack the dry food into one large container and put everything that needs to stay cool in a cool box. Take a second cool box for beverages so you can get to everything easily. It's a good idea to pack things in the cool box in the order you'll need them. Test your stove before you leave.

Organise your gear into large, clear plastic tubs that fit snugly into your car's trunk – again, it's a good idea to pack things in the order you'll need them. Fill up a tub with your kitchen gear and pack separate tubs for lighting equipment, such as lanterns and matches, and washing up. Once you're done with packing, label your tubs. Use a utensil/tool roll to protect knives and a multi-compartment plastic toolbox for other handy bits like bottle openers, tools and rubber bands. Large tote bags are also a good idea, as they are easy to access and carry.

Take a spare set of car keys and keep them somewhere safe, along with an extra torch (flashlight). Leave an extra lighter in your glovebox to make sure it stays dry.

Pack your vehicle systematically so that you can access essentials like your tent, lighting and wet weather gear easily as you start to unpack.

HOW TO PACK FOR A CAR CAMPING TRIP

Camping may be one of the best ways to connect with nature, but it requires foresight and planning – and a good checklist. This list will help ensure that you have a comfortable campsite and that you leave no trace of your visit behind.

Shelter, sleeping and relaxing
- Tent (double check you have your poles, pegs, guylines and spares)
- Mallet with a heavy, metal head
- Sleeping pads like the Exped MegaMat or an inflatable mattress
- Sleeping bag, blankets and/or a doona (comforter)
- Pillows
- Headlamps and a torch (flashlight), as well as extra batteries
- Camp chairs and a foldable, lightweight table
- Lanterns, such as a kerosene storm lantern and a battery lantern
- Hard-wearing picnic rug and blankets

Cooking and the fire
- Stove and fuel
- Two cool boxes (one for beverages and one for food) and ice
- Drinking water and an easy-to-fill container for collecting water onsite
- Water filter or treatment tablets
- Funnel
- Lighters and matches (stored in waterproof containers)
- Charcoal (with firestarter)
- Firewood and kindling (always check to see if you are allowed to collect wood at the site)
- Frying pan (a 25.5 cm/10 in pan is ideal)

- Favourite camp coffee-making device, like an Aeropress (see *How to make the perfect campfire brew* on page 16)
- Cooking pots (don't take your favourites; get camping pots from a second-hand store)
- Plates, bowls, mixing bowls and mugs (bamboo, BPA-free plastics or enamel are a good investment)
- Utensils such as a chef/chopping knife, paring knife, serving spoon, cutlery and long metal skewers, and a utensil roll for safely transporting them
- Barbecue spatula and fork
- Chopping board
- Cooking oil or spray
- Condiments, salt and pepper
- Foil and plastic wrap
- Vacuum bottle/thermos
- Water bottles
- Tupperware or airtight food containers
- Resealable plastic storage bags
- Rubbish bags

Useful tools

- Fixed-blade knife (this needs to be sharp and in its sheath when not in use)
- Saw or axe/hatchet (folding saws are a very handy camp tool for cutting wood for fuel – see *How to chop firewood* on page 8)
- Foldable shovel with sharp blade (great for digging out car wheels, creating a fire pit, tending the fire or digging a latrine)
- Multi-tool or Swiss Army knife that includes a knife, bottle opener, corkscrew and can opener
- Gaffer tape
- Rope or paracord (some of its many uses include washing line and tarp ridgelines)
- Carabiners and adjustable webbing straps (you will find many uses for these)

Washing up and cleaning

- Collapsible washing-up tub
- Biodegradable soap
- Steel scrubs and sponges
- Collapsible water container(s)
- Kitchen towels
- Tea towels
- Dust pan and brush (helpful for keeping the tent free of dirt)
- Bucket with lid

Personal

- Toiletry bag with common-sense essentials
- Baby wipes and hand sanitiser
- Toilet paper in a resealable plastic bag
- Sunscreen, lip balm and insect repellent
- Towels

Miscellaneous

- Luggage (backpacks, tote bags, duffels and other soft bags are a good idea)
- Daypack

- Spare clothing, particularly for warmth (jackets, hoodies, beanie, shorts, socks, thermals, fleece, merino underwear, swimming gear – you never know how cold or wet things will get)
- Wet-weather gear
- Sun hat or cap with detachable mosquito/fly net
- Hiking boots or trail shoes
- Thongs (flip flops)
- Gloves (fingerless is a great way to stay warm and still accomplish things around camp)
- Maps and a compass
- Spare car key kept in a safe place
- Spare batteries and extra fuel for lantern(s) and stove
- Sunglasses
- Spare eyeglasses and contact lenses
- First aid kit with whistle, painkillers and rehydration packs
- Watch with an alarm

Not essential, but nice to have

- Griddle or grill rack for cooking on an open fire
- Shade tarp
- Hammock
- Mosquito/fly netting
- Dutch oven
- Camera
- Umbrella
- Binoculars
- Solar powered batteries (check out Goal Zero)
- Trekking poles
- Two-way radio set
- Bluetooth speaker (waterproof)
- Biking/kayaking/fishing gear

HOW TO CHOOSE A CAMPSITE

When it comes to picking your spot, learning what to look for and what to steer clear of is a crucial part of enjoying the experience. First, you need to figure out what kind of camping you're doing: established campground camping with facilities or a more remote adventure? From there, it's all about protection from the elements and a nice, flat piece of land.

If you've only camped one or two times before, plan to stay in an established campground. These will usually have amenities such as a designated fire pit, a picnic table and flushing toilets (sometimes even a shower). Try not to camp too close to the bathroom facilities, as they attract heavy traffic and produce strong odours – a site at least a short walk away will provide a much needed olfactory buffer zone.

For more experienced campers, a remote location or bush camp will give you more opportunities for seclusion and are the best way to experience nature's ambiance. It's best, however, to choose an established campsite in an official camping area so that you can minimise your impact on the landscape you've come so far to enjoy.

If you're out in the wild, choose a campsite near a river or other water source. Apart from giving you access to fresh drinking water (make sure you boil it first!), you'll also have a place to bathe (although you shouldn't use soap in rivers and lakes) and a water source for washing up, cooking and dousing fires. If you've got kids with you, be mindful of fast-flowing water.

Avoid camping in old riverbeds or gullies. Instead, look for a level piece of ground near a slope so water can run off in the event of rain. Think about the position of the sun and shade – the morning sun will dry a canvas tent, and ideally you'll want shade from the midday sun. However much you want shade, avoid camping under a tree – falling branches, critters and insects can make this hazardous.

Finally, choose a spot that is sheltered from prevailing winds. Remember, you can use your vehicle as shade or wind protection if you need it.

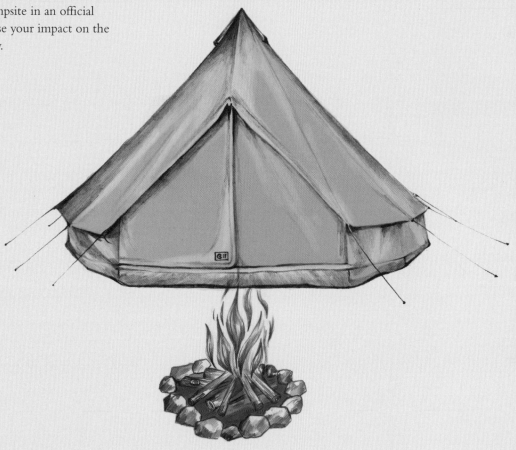

HOW TO SET UP A CAMPSITE

Organising your campsite is key to having a relaxed experience. Once it gets dark, you don't want to have to stumble around, tripping over random piles of equipment while you search in vain for this pot or that blanket. Camping is best enjoyed when everything has its designated place and is easy to lay your hands on when you need it.

The first thing to do after arriving at a campsite is set up your shelter and kitchen areas. Plan these spaces by laying your gear out on the ground. Try to keep your cooking, eating and washing up areas well away from your tent.

Choose a flat spot on which to pitch your tent (see *How to choose a campsite* on page 5). Remove any debris, such as rocks or sticks, that could damage your groundsheet or make for an uncomfortable stay. Pace out the size of your tent, making sure you have plenty of room on all sides for the guyropes.

Camping in the wild instead of in designated campgrounds might mean you have to build your own latrine area. Make sure this area is well away from your camp. Be mindful about hygiene and any potential water contamination issues. Most importantly, leave no trace – that means no toilet paper chucked in the latrine.

A fire pit is an essential for the full camping experience. Cooking on an open fire is one of life's great culinary experiences, and the campfire will be your main source of light and heat. If possible, use an existing fire circle that past campers have left behind. If you need to make one from scratch, choose an area of about 3 m (10 ft) in diameter that is free of flammable debris and grass – bare soil, sand or gravel is best. If you have a camp shovel, dig out a shallow circle, about 1 m (3 ft) wide, and place rocks around the circumference of your pit to ensure your fire doesn't spread (see *How to build a campfire* on page 10).

Keep your camp tidy to cut down on animals in your campsite and prevent you from tripping over things in the dark. You and your campmates should strive to develop good camp routines and habits, like washing up after eating and returning tools and equipment to their designated space. Keep all food and food waste in sealed containers that critters and insects can't access. If your campsite has bear boxes or other storage containers on site, use them.

If you foraged for your wood (see *How to chop firewood* on page 8), keep it handy in a designated area. Remember that freshly cut wood often needs to dry out. Proximity to the fire will help with this process, but be mindful that it can ignite if you're not careful.

Always put your fire out before going to sleep or leaving your site (see *How to build a campfire* on page 10).

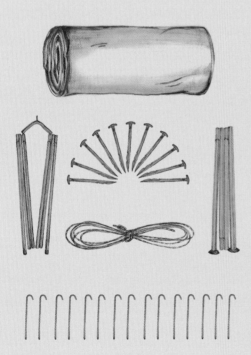

HOW TO TIE USEFUL CAMPING KNOTS

You don't have to know these simple knots to go camping, but they will prove helpful when it comes to everything from making sure your tent is securely anchored to stringing up a hammock. These classics have withstood the test of time and are very useful for a simple camping setup.

Bowline knot

The bowline knot, otherwise known as 'The King of Knots', is a classic fixed-loop knot used to secure an object to something else – whether that's securing a tarp or a hammock to a tree, or hanging up your food/kitchen gear where camp critters can't reach it. The bowline is particularly popular because it tightens under weight, doesn't slip and, when not supporting weight, is easy to tie and untie. It's a simple knot to learn, particularly if you memorise this well-known mnemonic: 'up through the rabbit hole, around the big tree; down through the rabbit hole and off goes he'.

Square (reef) knot

A good choice for joining two ropes of equal weight and thickness together, the square knot can be used to tie a bundle of kindling or secure rubbish bags. This knot is not suitable for supporting anything weighty (like a human) and will slip under tension.

Tautline hitch

The tautline hitch is a supremely clever knot, useful for securing tent or tarp guylines to pegs. It creates tension between the tent and the peg; when the tautline hitch has been tied correctly, it's easy to adjust the tension back and forth.

 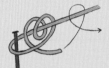

Timber hitch

The timber hitch is used to attach a length of rope to a cylindrical object such as a log. It's often used by arborists or woodsmen to drag or tow a bundle of logs, as it will tighten with strain and lets go easily when that strain eases.

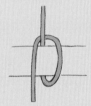  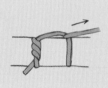

Double half (clove) hitch

This is a practical, easy-to-learn knot whose main function is securing a rope directly to an object, often a branch, log or post. The double half hitch can be used to tether animals or secure a tarp or hammock, but it can slip if it isn't under enough tension.

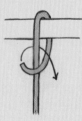  

HOW TO CHOP FIREWOOD

There's something satisfying, almost primeval, about swinging an axe and splitting a log, about feeling the rasp of the wood against your palm and splinters in your fingers as you pile the chopped wood high ready for seasoning. It's an achievement, being ready for winter, knowing you'll be able to sit around a roaring home or campfire, feeding it log after log, as you share meals and stories around its warmth.

You will need:
good-quality axe
chopping block (or tree stump)
sturdy footwear
logs

Collecting wood
Unless you plan on taking bulk wood with you, you'll no doubt be foraging for fuel wood for a campfire. Before you leave you should research the rules in the area where you're planning to camp. Chopping down a tree or collecting fallen branches isn't always legal, especially in national parks, so it pays to check before you leave.

It should go without saying that you'll want to look for dry, dead wood that you'll process into a combination of sizes for kindling and larger fuel logs. When wood has dried and its moisture and sap has evaporated, it's known as 'seasoned wood', as opposed to 'greenwood' (live wood) where internal moisture is at its maximum.

Ideally, you'll be on the lookout for a combination of softwoods and hardwoods. Softwoods to get the fire blazing, and hardwoods to carry it through the night and produce heat.

Preparing your logs
Once you've collected your wood, you may need to chop it into smaller logs or 'rounds' – in other words, break it down into smaller pieces that will be easier to split (not pictured). A saw is the best tool for the job. Your logs need to be short enough to fit into a fire pit or wood stove. When in doubt, about 30–40cm (12–16in) is a good size. You'll also want to even out the ends of each log so that it can stand up straight – a necessity for chopping wood.

Positioning your logs
When you're chopping wood, you'll need a raised flat surface or stump. In an ideal world, you'd have a dry stump between 30cm (12in) and knee height. If this isn't available, try to find a large downed tree lying in a horizontal position that has enough flat surface area to safely balance the log.

Place the log on top of the stump on the far side away from you, so that if you miss your axe head will definitely end up hitting the stump. Make sure the log is standing up straight and not about to fall over.

Take your time to get the right position – this is not a job that should be rushed. Before you begin swinging an axe, ensure that your axe swing will not be inhibited by other objects, like branches (or people!). Keep your feet shoulder-width apart, squarely facing the stump. Make sure your stance is weighted evenly, with your legs and arms slightly bent and fairly relaxed.

Positioning your logs

Holding your axe

With your axe in both hands, hold the axe horizontally at waist level, using your dominant hand to grip the handle near to the axe head. The V of your hand should be facing away from you. Use your other (non-dominant) hand to grip the other end near to the handle.

Taking a swing

Check the striking distance to the log by lining up your axe with the target and tapping the log in the spot that you're aiming for. Aim for existing cracks on the edge of the wood which will help direct your first strike and ensure that you're less likely to get your axe stuck in the round.

As you swing the axe back and up, extend your arms high over your head, straighten your legs, then rise up slightly on the balls of your feet to maximise the swing. When your hands and axe are at arms-length, directly overhead and at the top of the arc, let the axe drop down towards the log with your eyes fixed steadily on the target. As you're doing this let your dominant hand slide down the handle to meet your other hand and apply some force on the downward stroke.

Chopping wood isn't about being aggressive. Accuracy and technique are far more important than brute force. Use the axe's weight to your advantage and let the tool do the work for you.

Chopping to size

Depending on the size of your logs, you may need to split them in half or into quarters. After splitting in half, reposition one half of your log on the chopping block and split that in half. Repeat with the other half of the log.

Stacking and seasoning

If you're cutting firewood for at-home use, you want to stack it where it will be protected from the elements, but also where the sun will dry the moisture from the logs – this process is called seasoning. Ideally you want to cut, split and stack your firewood in early spring to give it time to fully season. Depending on your location and climate, this could take anywhere from six months to a year. If you're in a rainy area, cover your firewood a few weeks before you plan to use it.

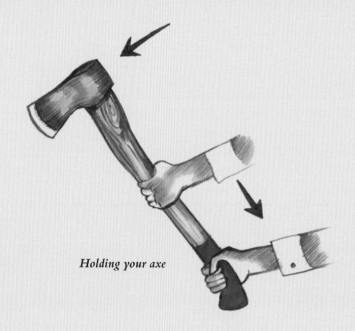

Holding your axe

Taking a swing

Stacking and seasoning

HOW TO BUILD A CAMPFIRE

A roaring campfire is essential when you're spending a night in the bush. It does more than ward off the dark and any inquisitive animals; it's the heart of the campsite. The place where you'll gather to stay warm, cook and swap stories long into the night, until the fire is nothing more than smouldering embers.

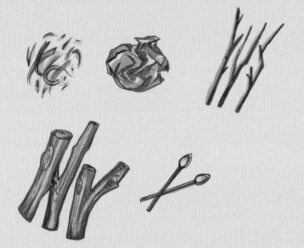

You will need:
shovel (for digging your fire pit and moving hot coals)
newspaper and woodchips
*kindling (thin twigs and branches around the length
   of a drinking straw)*
tinder (light, dry fuel such as bark and woodchips)
fuelwood (thicker branches, preferably dead fallen logs)
matches

Picking the fire's location
You'll need to set up your fire well before dark so you can see what you're doing, a process that starts by selecting your campfire's location. Most campsites will have fire pits or cleared patches of ground where others have set up campfires. If you have to create your own, choose the location carefully; it should be clear of anything that might catch (like brush or dry grass) and have no overhanging branches. Dig a hole around 10 cm (4 in) deep and 1 m (3 ft) wide and surround it with a wide circle of rocks to keep the fire from spreading.

Preparing your tinder and kindling
Place loosely scrunched newspaper and tinder in the centre of the fire pit. When foraging for tinder, look for soft wood, dry bark, small twigs, pinecones or pine needles. You could use a sharp knife to pare fine strips of softwood or shred the bark (see *How to chop firewood* on page 8). Make sure your tinder is dry or you'll get a fire that smokes a lot and not much else.

Lodge one thick stick into the ground at the centre of your fire. Lean your kindling in a loose teepee shape against it, around the pile of tinder.

Lighting your fire
Light the paper and tinder in a few places around the teepee. Gradually add more kindling, placing it using the same teepee formation as before. Blow on the base of the fire to add oxygen and build the flames. Once your fire is crackling merrily, add the fuelwood around the base of the teepee. Don't add the fuelwood too quickly, as this can smother the fire – start with two logs on opposite sides of the fire and build up.

Putting out your fire
Let your fire burn down to ashes before gently dousing it with water; the fire may hiss and smoke, so don't stand too close. Keep pouring water onto the fire until the hissing stops. Mix the embers together with a shovel until everything is wet. Once everything is wet, reach in and feel the ashes. They should be cold to the touch. Pick up the rocks on the edge of your fire circle and feel the ground underneath. If anything still feels warm, you need to continue watering the fire. Once your fire is doused to your satisfaction, scour the surrounding ground for any embers or sparks. If water is in short supply, bury the remains of your fire with dirt or sand.

HOW TO SPIT ROAST

Slowly cooking a joint of meat over an open fire is, for some, the pinnacle of primitive camp cooking. Using a portable spit roaster – or better yet, a spit you have fashioned from a hardwood branch – is a sure-fire way to impress your fellow campers. The slowly turning meat will self-baste, resulting in a sweetly charred, succulent roast that's full of flavour.

Building the spit
Take some fresh green wood from a nearby tree to make your single-use spit roast. Look for a branch from a hardwood tree – you are looking for a straight piece with a kink at one end, which will become the 'crank' of the spit. Choose one about 3 cm (1 in) thick; the ideal length will depend on the size of your cut of meat.

Using a sharp hunting knife, hatchet or machete, remove the side branches and pare off the bark. Sharpen the end (the one without the crank) to a point.

Supporting the spit
Find two strong branches with Y forks at one end, which will be what supports your spit. These branches will ideally be at least 25 cm (10 in) from the foot to the fork, and at least 3 cm (1 in) thick.

Remove the bark from both sticks and sharpen the foot ends to a point.

Using a mallet, drive the supporting forks into the earth at the appropriate distance to leave about 10 cm (4 in) of your spit at each end.

You will need:
1 butterflied lamb, rolled boneless beef, tenderloin roast, rolled pork loin, whole chicken or rabbit (1.5 to 2 kg/3½ to 4½ lb)
2 garlic cloves, finely chopped or crushed
handful of fresh herbs such as rosemary and sage, chopped or crushed
zest of one lemon
1 tsp sea salt
freshly ground black pepper
4 tbsp olive oil

If you are feeding a lot of people, you might use the whole animal – lamb or pig are a good bet. You will need to adjust the size of your spit accordingly.

Preparing the meat
Bring the meat to room temperature. Place it in a plastic bag or mixing bowl. In a separate bowl, mix the garlic, herbs, lemon zest, salt, pepper and oil. Add half of this mixture to the bag or mixing bowl with the meat, ensuring it is evenly covered.

Using the sharp end of the spit, penetrate the meat lengthwise from end to end. You might want to use a skewer or two to ensure the meat is secured to the spit. If you are roasting a rolled beef or butterflied lamb, then use cooking twine to hold it together.

Cooking the meat
About an hour before you start cooking, build a fire near your spit setup. Make sure your fire is producing plenty of hot coals before you start cooking your meat.

Attach your meat spit to the supporting Y forks – your spit should be about 15 cm (6 in) away from the coalbed.

Place a cast-iron pan filled with generous splashes of water and wine beneath your meat – it will collect the meat's drippings to make gravy later and help prevent fire flare-ups.

Using your shovel, start to build a hot coalbed around the dripping pan and between the supporting forks. You will start to notice your meat sizzling slowly. As it starts to change colour, use the crank to turn it every now and again. Baste the meat occasionally with the remainder of your herb marinade.

Here's a tip: it's a good idea to maintain your main fire so that you have a steady supply of hot coals at hand. You can control the pace of your cooking by moving your coalbed towards or away from the meat.

Cooking time will depend on the size and type of your meat cut, but expect to cook for at least an hour – the slower, the better. Watch your campmates melt with anticipation as the meat nears cooked perfection. Serve with fire-roasted veggies, gravy and a good beverage.

HOW TO COOK ON AN OPEN FIRE

There are many ways to cook on an open fire. With a minimum of tools – all you really need is a stick – you can hold food at the optimum distance from heat in order to crisp or roast it. As you expand your culinary range, include stews, casseroles and fry-ups, or increase the size of your portions with larger cuts of meat, you will need to invest in some tools and utensils to manage open-fire cooking.

Equipment to use over open flames

Pots, skillets and saucepans: Cast-iron is our preference for cooking on an open fire, as it's durable, heats evenly and can handle extreme temperatures. Cast-iron is heavy, though, so its not recommended for lightweight camping adventures.

Dutch (camp) ovens: A Dutch oven is a large pot with a lid and legs. The best ones are made of cast-iron and may well be the only camp cookware you will ever need. The advantage of a Dutch oven is its versatility; you can reproduce just about any one-pot dish that you could make at home on your kitchen stove. Dutch ovens retain and distribute heat evenly, which means less chance of burning your food. It offers a tremendous amount of control with cooking, as you can cover the oven with coals or move it further away from the heat source when needed.

Grills and griddle plates: A grill is a metal grate that will support your food at the right distance from the coal bed. Having a stable, flat surface is handy for pots, pans and kettles. You can adjust the height of the grill or move the coals into different layers beneath the grill to control the heat. Griddle plates are great for cooking smaller pieces of meat (rashers, chops, chicken) or veggies without them falling through into the fire.

Other bits of useful camp cooking kit

Fireproof mitts or gloves: Getting close to hot fires can easily lead to burns. A pair of fireproof mitts or gloves are essential for safe campfire cooking.

Long-handled spoon or fork: Used to prod food, remove lids from pots and move coals around the fire.

Shovel: Used for digging a fire pit and moving hot coals around.

Building a fire hot enough for roasting

Build and light your fire (see *How to build a campfire* on page 10). When building a fire to roast food, it pays to have some hardwood on hand. Hardwood is the best fuel for producing extremely hot coals, which will be crucial for roasting and grilling. Try to have your hardwood chopped to kindling size, as smaller pieces of wood will burn down to coals more quickly (see *How to chop firewood* on page 8). Building a second, and even a third, fire with kindling tipis is a great way to get your cooking fire producing coal quickly.

After your fire has burnt for about half an hour, the flames will start reducing and your fire will begin producing hot coals. These will give off an even heat, which you can control by moving around your cookware, spit or grill. At this stage, you will need to be vigilant about continuing to stoke the fire's heat with fresh fuel.

Using a long-handled spoon or shovel, you can isolate the hot coals and move them to the side that will become your cooking fire. You can keep adding more kindling to the main fire, as this will keep producing hot coals for your cooking fire.

You now have the option of either cooking directly on the coals, using a pot or skillet, or setting up a grill, or even a spit.

Roasting some veggies

Some vegetables are perfect for roasting in a campfire with little or no preparation or tools. You can simply bury veggies such as potatoes, sweet potatoes, butternut pumpkin (squash), Jerusalem artichokes, turnips, chestnuts, garlic and onions in the hot ashes, or set them near hot coals, for an hour or so. When you retrieve your treasure from the fire, simply peel away the outer layer or slice the veggie in half and spoon out its soft centre. If you want to keep the skin of your veggie intact, then wrap it in aluminium foil prior to cooking or, better yet, in soaked banana or palm leaves.

To roast corn ears, soak them in water for an hour, then place directly onto your hot coals. Cook for 30 minutes or so, turning a few times, and you will be rewarded with wonderfully charred husks and perfectly steamed corn. Just add butter, salt and pepper to achieve instant camp legend status.

If you want to get a little fancy, you can't beat Hasselback potatoes: crispy outer layers and beautifully soft, creamy centres make these a campfire favourite. Choose medium-sized roasting spuds. One by one, nestle the potatoes in the curve of a large wooden spoon. Using a sharp knife, slice downwards until your knife hits the edge of the spoon. Work the knife from one end of the potato to the other, spacing your slices about ½ cm (⅛ in) apart. Meanwhile, heat some oil and butter in a pan along with some thin slices of garlic. Brush your potatoes with the oil/butter/garlic mixture, then salt generously. Either wrap your spuds in foil or banana leaves, or arrange in your favourite cookware – a Dutch oven is great for this. You can add grated cheese and chives at the end for extra points.

HOW TO BAKE CAMPFIRE SODA BREAD IN A DUTCH OVEN

There's nothing quite as satisfying or simple as making soda bread over a crackling campfire. This classic Irish bread is known as damper in Australia and a bannock in Scotland – it tastes delicious wherever you make it (and whatever you call it). This recipe has few ingredients and very little preparation, yet will impress your fellow campers no end.

You will need:

2 cups flour (we use a combination of organic wholemeal and white flour – feel free to experiment)

1 tsp salt

1 level tsp bicarbonate of soda (baking soda)

1 cup buttermilk (or 1 cup milk mixed with 1 tbsp lemon juice)

100 g (3½ oz) butter, cold

3 tbsp honey

Optional add-ins:

⅓ cup mixed grain and seed blend, mixed in after you've blended the wet and dry ingredients: sunflower seeds, millet, pumpkin seeds, rolled oats, etc, to add some texture

¾ cup sourdough starter, added to the wet mix for a healthy, fermented bread

replace the buttermilk with probiotic yoghurt or even dark stout

Preparing the dough

Thoroughly combine flours, bicarbonate of soda and salt in a large bowl. We sieve these ingredients together at home and take them camping in a resealable plastic bag or container.

Put the buttermilk in a medium bowl. In a small pan, warm the butter by the fire until soft, then pour it into the buttermilk. Stir in the honey and mix everything together until well combined.

Make a well in the centre of the dry flour mix and slowly pour the wet mix into it. Stir with a wooden spoon for about a minute until the mixture comes together – stir steadily, but not vigorously. If the mix is too dry to form a dough, add a tablespoon or two of milk or water.

Spoon the mix onto a lightly floured surface, such as a chopping board, then knead the dough with floured hands until you achieve a soft and almost fluffy texture.

Don't overdo the kneading – just four or five kneads should be enough. The bi-carb soda and buttermilk will react as soon as they meet, and minimal handling will help preserve this reaction. The idea is to get the bread into the Dutch oven while that reaction is still going strong, which means as quickly as possible.

Shape the mixture into a ball, then flatten slightly using the palm of your hand.

Dip a knife in flour and make a deep cross through the centre of the bread, extending each line out to the dough's edges. This will make it easy to break the bread into quarters after it is baked.

Prepping the fire and Dutch oven

The key to cooking bread in a Dutch oven is getting a consistent temperature around the whole pot (see *How to cook on an open fire* on page 12). Make sure your campfire includes plenty of hardwood that had been burning long enough to produce a good number of hot coals.

Using a kitchen towel or newspaper, wipe the inside of your Dutch oven with a thin coating of oil or butter, then dust with flour.

Preheat the Dutch oven by placing it directly on the bed of hot coals. Nestle the ball of dough in the centre of the oven. Put the lid on the pot, making sure no steam is escaping. Push the Dutch oven down into the bed of coals, then use a shovel to cover the lid with coals and embers. You may need to repeat this process during the bake.

Baking and finishing

Bake until the crust is golden brown. The cooking time depends on how hot your coals are, but it generally takes 25 to 35 minutes. To see if your bread is baked, push a knife into the middle of the loaf; if the knife comes out clean, then the bread is done. If the knife comes out wet, with some bread dough sticking to it, then it needs more time. When done, it will also sound hollow when tapped underneath. This bread tastes great even if it's a little under- or overdone, so you don't need to worry about the bake being perfect.

Remove the bread from the oven, brush the top with butter and let it cool under a moist tea towel. Eat as soon as possible with a hearty meal.

HOW TO MAKE THE PERFECT CAMPFIRE BREW

The familiar process of preparing coffee in the morning increases in significance when it happens in the outdoors. The whole process is warming, comforting. The resulting cup of coffee – cradled in your hands as you watch the sunrise – is so much more satisfying. This method for preparing a campfire coffee uses the easily transportable Aeropress, which produces the perfect filter brew.

You will need:
½ litre (17 fl oz) water
Aeropress with filter
fresh coffee beans
coffee grinder
digital scale
timer

Prepping your coffee
Bring at least half a litre (17 fl oz) of fresh water to a boil over the campfire. While you're waiting for the water to boil, measure out 15 g (½ oz) of coffee and grind it to the consistency of table salt or course sand.

Rinse the Aeropress chamber and the filter with the hot water, and warm up your cup with the hot water while you're at it. Save 200 g (7 oz) of hot water for making your coffee. Discard the water from your chamber and filter once you're done.

Setting up your Aeropress
Assemble your Aeropress by pushing the plunger, seal first, slightly into the chamber at the opposite end to where you'll twist on the filter cap. Place your scale on a flat and steady surface, then place the Aeropress on top with the plunger section on the bottom. Add your ground coffee to the top of the seal in the chamber. Tare your scales to zero.

Starting your brew
Add 200 g (7 oz) of boiling water to the ground coffee and start your timer. After one minute, give the brew a good stir. Let it steep for another minute. Place your filter into the filter cap, then attach it to the top of the chamber and twist it in.

Flipping your brew
Place your cup over the filter cap. Very carefully, turn the Aeropress upside down so your cup is now on the scale (or another bit of steady, flat ground).

Filtering your brew
Gently and slowly press the plunger down until the brew is completely pushed through the paper filter. Sit back and enjoy.

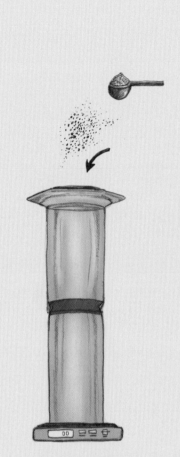

Setting up your Aeropress

Starting your brew

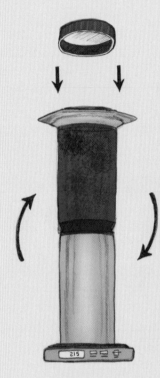

Flipping your brew

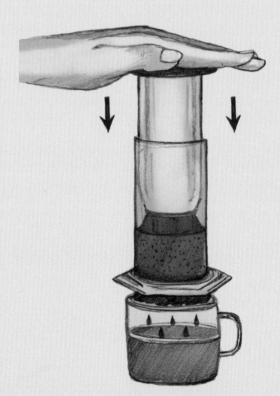

Filtering your brew

Enjoy!

HOW TO MAKE A FORAGED ROSE COCKTAIL

There are few things the forager loves more than an invasive species; the more you pick, the more virtuous you feel. *Rosa rugosa*, a salt-tolerant rose native to eastern Asia, has been making an increasing nuisance of itself on several continents after escaping from gardens where it is used to form a colourful hedge. It has taken over large areas of Europe, notably in coastal regions, and is also found extensively in North America and in the more urban reaches of Australasia. You may even have one in your garden.

Almost any rose, cultivated or wild, can be useful in the kitchen, but *Rosa rugosa* has two exceptional qualities – gorgeously fragrant petals and large hips ('hips' being the bright red fruits that form after the petals have fallen). The petals bear the quintessential perfume of roses, which lends itself to clear spirits like vodka, while the hips form the basis of a wonderful sweetener called rosehip syrup.

You will need:

small basketful of Rosa rugosa *petals*
bottle of vodka or eau de vie (fruit brandy)

small basketful of Rosa rugosa *hips*
water (enough to cover the rose hips)
caster sugar

Making rose petal spirit

Rosa rugosa has a long season and the plant continues to produce petals while other flowers set into hips. Pluck the petals from the green parts of the flower just as they are opening (to avoid the angry bee likely to be found inside). A small basketful of petals should be enough. Pack them inside a glass jar, pressing down gently. Put the lid on the jar and leave them at room temperature for 24 hours. Top up the jar with a good-quality vodka or eau de vie, put the top back on and leave for a week. Using a fine-mesh strainer or muslin, strain the liquor into sealable bottles, squeezing the petals so that no liquid is wasted. You won't know whether to drink this rose petal vodka or dab it behind your ears.

Making rosehip syrup

Wait for the hips to become red and ripe, then snap off enough to fill a small basket. Place in a medium-sized saucepan and fill it with just enough water to cover the hips. Boil them until the hips are soft. Gently mash the contents of the pan with a potato masher, then squeeze through a very fine mesh straining bag. Wash the bag and strain once more to ensure that none of the stomach-irritating hairs that adorn the seeds remain (children have long used rosehip seeds as itching powder). Heat the puree with a substantial amount of sugar – you can experiment with the amount, but a 1:1 sugar to puree ratio works well – and you will have rosehip syrup. It can be kept for two weeks in the fridge, or you can bottle and store or freeze it.

Making rose petal cocktails

Rose petal spirit is a bit of a trial to drink on its own, but wonderful in mixes and cocktails. I make a lot of wild cocktails, and I sometimes spray a glass with the rose petal vodka to give the whole thing a rosy perfume. Stirred into a chilled glass of your rosehip syrup, it is a summer evening treat.

The best summer cocktail I have ever tried (my own proud invention – you are welcome) is called a Pink Pint. I will leave the quantities to your own fine judgement, but the ingredients are: rose petal vodka, rosehip syrup, raspberry juice, lemonade (lemon-lime soda, for Americans), soda water and ice. Cheers!

John Wright, who shared this recipe, is a forager who lives in England. He shares his skills and knowledge of foraging on the coast and in the forest sustainably, often through his work with River Cottage, an organisation that promotes healthy eating and sustainable agriculture.

HOW (AND WHY) TO CAMP SUSTAINABLY

Camping offers opportunities to see and experience a new landscape, to forage from new fields and connect with local growers. It's possible to be even more sustainable on the road than it is at home, if you know how to pack and what to search for while you're out on adventures.

The experience of camping can change so much depending on how you do it. For us, the best camping experience comes when you totally immerse yourself in your environment, in the culture and nature around you – it makes for a much more sustainable experience.

It's about collecting food from where you are, both wild and locally produced, and choosing camp spots that are abundant with resources, like wood for your fire and water for your pot. It's about bringing the essential items with you so that you have everything you need to be comfortable, but leaving everything else behind so that you have to forage from the local landscape as you adventure through it.

Of course, sustainability isn't just about nature. It's about respecting the place you are visiting as a whole, which includes the people who live in it. The best way we've found to do this is to support local producers and buy fresh, local food from them. This food is always the best and it has no carbon miles attached to it. Plus you get to interact with local people who can help you identify good spots to fish, or to forage wild fruits or mushrooms. Support local communities and they'll support you.

When driving around, observe what is abundant around you, like crops, roadside stalls or local sourdough bakeries. There's almost always a local farmers market, usually on the weekend. And if you talk to locals, you'll often find someone with a verdant garden who will sell or trade you something! Keep your eyes peeled as you drive along too – food is all around us.

Camping sustainably is really that simple. If we don't respect the natural environment and the local people, enjoyable camping experiences will soon be a thing of the past. But respect both of these and we guarantee you and future campers will continue to wish you never had to go home.

Packing smart
Camping is a simple time, one made for getting back to basics. The only two essential tasks you need to worry about are gathering food … and then eating it! How we perform these two simple tasks makes all the difference between camping sustainably and just camping.

Food essentials
We bring just the basics and source the vast majority of our food locally. We always set out with:

- Some homemade passata.

- A jam or marmalade.

- Some pickled mixed vegetables and some fermented vegetables like dill pickles or kimchi (to keep our bellies healthy while we travel).

- Nuts and seeds.

- Pumpkin, potatoes, sweet potatoes, ginger, turmeric, garlic. These are versatile fresh foods that store super well for a long time without refrigeration and easily add flavour to so many different meals!

- Unrefined salt and pepper.

- Good olive oil for cooking.

We generally cook on the fire and it's super important to bring the right equipment for this; otherwise camp cooking can be a major time- and energy-sucker. It only takes a small fire to stay warm and if you have the right equipment, a small fire is all you'll need for cooking as well.

Equipment
There's no need to get too carried away and bring everything, including the kitchen sink, on the road. Again, camping should be a simple time. Here are a few essentials we always pack:

- Two stainless steel billies. As steel heats up fast, it is the most efficient vessel in which to boil water.

- A cast-iron frying pan and Dutch (camp) oven. Cast-iron stores heat; this is the most efficient way to capture your fire's peak energy when cooking more intensive meals.

- A thermos. This means you can make the day's tea/coffee and hot food on just one fire, whenever it suits you best – and keep it hot all day! We even have two small 330 ml (11 fl oz) thermoses for takeaway coffees on the go because they last a lifetime compared to regular reusable coffee cups.

- Coffee grinder and maker (plunger, Aeropress, stovetop – whatever you're into!).

- A good shovel. Your all-purpose camp tool for moving coals, digging toilet holes and a million other little tasks, but, most importantly, for burying all your compostable scraps to keep them out of landfill. Always bury toilet and food waste at least 20 centimetres (8 in) deep and away from water sources.

- A quality esky (cool box). Spend on this. A good esky will stay cold with just one bag of ice for up to a week!

Here's a tip: forget the soap. When you're done cooking, if you have a greasy pot, throw in some wood ash and water and leave it overnight. The combination of fat and ash will make soap overnight, which you can heat to do your dishes with in the morning.

Gathering the local abundance

Wild foods can vary greatly from place to place,* but some super-common things to look out for on the road are:

- Wild fennel. An awesome flavouring for soups, stews, etc.

- Wild apples, plums and figs. These look exactly the same as the regular ones, but are just growing wild!

- Blackberries and other wild berries. Make sure they haven't been sprayed. Roadsides invariably are, but deep bush is generally safe – just make sure there is no yellowing of the leaves, which is a sure sign you need to move on.

- Fish (and other game too, though fishing is by far the simplest way to gather wild meat).**

* Don't gather from the wild without the supervision of an experienced mentor.

** Make sure you get a fishing/game licence for the state you are in.

Matt and Lentil Purbrick live a sustainable life on their farm, growing and harvesting and planting in rhythm with nature's seasons (see page 145).

HOW TO LEAVE NO TRACE

The most important part of camping – of any outdoor activity, really – is ensuring you leave nature just as you found her. That means travelling carefully: driving and walking on already established paths to minimise damage; being mindful about where you're going; taking your gear and rubbish away with you when you leave; and replacing anything you moved around. It's as simple as it sounds, but here are a few guidelines for successfully following the 'leave no trace' manifesto.

When hiking, plan your route and prepare properly for the terrain you will encounter. Knowing where you're heading means it's less likely you'll have to go off the established path. When hiking, don't spit seeds onto the ground or pick any flowers – anything that changes the natural environment is best avoided.

Set up your campsite on an already established spot. If that's not possible, choose a site that has already been cleared of vegetation and a few metres away from a water source to avoid contaminating the water with your washing up or personal care. If you use any rocks to anchor your tent, replace them when you leave.

Organise your food in advance so you have only exactly what you need; this way, you won't have to cart out much food waste, and you'll be less likely to leave something behind (see *How to pack for a car camping trip* on page 3).

Use existing fire pits where possible and keep your fire small. Be careful with campfires – set up the fire properly within a fire ring, make sure someone is always watching the fire and that it stays small and manageable. When you leave the campsite, ensure the fire is properly extinguished (see *How to build a campfire* on page 10).

Don't wash your kitchenware in the nearby water source – if you do need to use the water, collect some from the creek, river or lake and take it back to your campsite. Most leave no trace manifestos say not to bathe in a river or lake, but if you do want to freshen up in a water source, do it without soap, which is a chemical product that will contaminate the water. Make sure you're around 50 m (164 ft) away from any rivers, lakes or oceans when using water containing soap or waste. Scatter the water around your campsite when you're done to ensure none of it runs into the water source.

Dispose of all human waste properly – that means away from water, buried deep in the ground. The further away from water, the better, as water contaminated by human waste leads to diseases like Giardia. Bury your toilet paper with the waste, but take any tampons or pads out with you.

Admire wildlife from a distance rather than giving them food or attention. Make sure to lock up your perishables and put them in a place that animals can't reach, otherwise you risk them trashing your campsite in search of food.

Walk in – and out – with a clean tent. Brushing down your tent and your shoes before you leave avoids passing soil-borne diseases from place to place.

Before you leave, thoroughly check the campsite for any trace of your visit. Collect rubbish that other, less vigilant campers may have left behind.

The rewards of awareness

When renowned photographer Christopher Phillips caught a bacterial infection called meningococcal during a trip to Bolivia, it changed his life. Struggling with treatment and recovery back home in Australia, Christopher started to practise meditation. It transformed not just his healing process, but his life and work. He found that his meditative practice made him a better photographer: his attention was heightened, his senses sharper, his patience wider. He now leads workshops on meditative photography in natural spaces.

The idea of combining meditation with nature and photography came to me after I contracted meningococcal. I had volunteered to work at an animal refuge in the Amazon basin, and I picked up the bacteria through the water supply.

Upon returning to Australia, I spent two years being treated by Western medicine with little results. So I started on an alternative therapy journey, which introduced me to Ayurveda medical practices and meditation.

My first week of meditating created both a mental and a physical shift. My body felt like it was cooling down after a lifetime of being agitated and out of alignment. My mind felt like it was quietly opening and relaxing, allowing me to see aspects of my life that had been hidden, into parts of myself I hadn't been able to see before.

This experience had profound implications for both my photography and my daily life. Whenever I meditated before the beginning of a shoot, I noticed myself becoming aware of far more than I had previously. I had a feeling that I was becoming part of each moment in a direct and connected way. My patience was extended, my vision heightened and my connection with the subject intensified.

I continued experimenting with this mix of meditation and photography and found that being in nature amplified my feeling of connection. Nature has fewer distractions and more invitations to be curious and engaged in the moment; the feeling of connecting with nature's patient, nonresistant vibrancy allowed me to tune in. The more I practised, the more this quality became part of my day-to-day.

I started getting up before dawn to drive to a national park, leaving just enough time to meditate in my car before the first rays of the sun appeared. Slowly, I'd begin exploring the new landscape, allowing all the sights, sounds and smells of the forest to lull me out of my mind, immersing me completely in the experience of observation. These sessions of meditative practice in nature left me feeling relaxed, focused and fulfilled.

> "
> Nature has fewer distractions and more invitations to be curious and engaged in the moment; the feeling of connecting with nature's patient, nonresistant vibrancy allowed me to tune in.

The focused awareness required for photography allowed me to penetrate more deeply. I noticed that it added structure to my practice, further refining my awareness so I could drop even more deeply into the moment. I refined my awareness so that my focus was on the fundamental elements of photography: highlights and shadows, colour, form and texture. To keep myself anchored to the present moment, I would continually bring my awareness back to the sensations of my body, starting with my hands, feet and the places where my clothes touched my body. As I became more focused and sensitive, I refined it to just the sensation of my breath entering and leaving my nostrils.

My feeling of being acutely aware began to strengthen; I could focus on what I was photographing, but I also had another level of consciousness that was observing everything I was doing. This regular practice of taking time to quieten my mind, to remove the judging, analytical side of thought and settle into nature's vibrant frequencies began to create changes. Not only in the quality of my photography, but in the quality and depth of my connection to life.

..........x

"

I'd begin exploring the new landscape, allowing all the sights, sounds and smells of the forest to lull me out of my mind, immersing me completely in the experience of observation.

Home is where you park it

Mitch Williams became obsessed with Volkswagen vans after watching classic '70s surfing movies. He always dreamed of the van life, planning how he would make the bed, how he would maximise the storage. He eventually purchased a classic four-speed column-shift manual 1978 Nissan e20 van, and after making it into a functioning tiny home, lived in it with his girlfriend. They winnowed life down to its simplest pleasures and material necessities, woke to the sunrise every morning and balanced time in nature with his day-to-day life as a graphic designer in Melbourne, Australia.

Tell us about your van.

Growing up I was obsessed with Kombi vans. Every Christmas and birthday I was swamped with Kombi-related mugs, cushions, t-shirts, key rings – even a Volkswagen hub cap. I was looking seriously at getting a van for about a year before I bought the 1978 Nissan e20, doing research and talking to mates with vans. The only thing I knew was that I wanted it to be retro (preferably '70s), just like the ones in the old surf movies I love, like *Morning of the Earth* and *The Endless Summer*. Those guys were living the dream.

The van runs really well for its age, even though it sometimes struggles getting up hills and going into reverse (the gears are pretty sticky). It's one of those motors that you drive by how it sounds and feels. If it's revving heaps, you back it off a bit and let it coast; if your seat starts heating up, it means the motor's getting hot – talk about '70s heated seats! It's frustrating at times, but that's the beauty of these old things. Treat them right and there's no reason for them to stop running.

What inspired you to get a van?

Well, the old surf films. And I really loved the idea of pulling up along the coast and waking up to check the surf every morning without getting out of bed. It's like having a beachfront house at all of my favourite surf spots. A room with a view – who wouldn't want that?

Have you spent any time living in the van, and how did it change the way you live?

Right after I bought the van, my girlfriend and I lived in it for two months on a farm in the Yarra Valley in Victoria, Australia. We loved waking up to the sunrise, no alarms; the sun would shine right through our window and we'd just wake up! Moving into the van meant we had to ditch almost everything we had down to strictly what we'd need on a day-to-day basis: some clothes, a couple of pairs of shoes, speakers, skateboards, surfboards, wetsuits, a guitar, a coffee grinder and a French press. Not to mention the little things to make it as homey as possible: plants, incense, books, pictures and *don't forget the mosquito spray!* Becoming a full-time van lifer and living the simple life is quite liberating; it's super humbling being surrounded by everything I need to be happy.

What's the best moment you've had in the van?

We've had so many awesome moments in the van. I'll always remember the first trip we took, down the Great Ocean Road. It had been my dream to drive it in my own van and it was surreal to actually be doing it: stopping and surfing when we found a wave and setting up camp with the views we'd only ever enjoyed in passing. It was a killer start to having the van.

What does van life mean to you?

Van life is all about not being tied down to one place. It's constantly being on an adventure and enjoying the things you really love. Van life is the ultimate freedom. For me, it became about letting go of my long-term plans and taking a step back to see my future from a different perspective. It's stressful at times, but allowing life to happen and being able to roll along with it (literally) is so much more exciting.

Being able to go with the flow opens up so many opportunities. I'm picking up new hobbies on the road: cooking, hiking, biking, exploring, popping into vintage stores and op-shops to find unique things for the van, photography, film, reading and road trip singalongs. Van life has made me appreciate those little awesome moments in life that you take for granted or that are easy to forget about: cooking outdoors, seeing sunrises and sunsets, rolling out of bed and instantly being outside (which really wakes you up), using candles for light and not just for smell, and falling asleep gazing up at the stars.

..........x

"

Van life is all about not being tied down to one place. It's constantly being on an adventure and enjoying the things you really love. Van life is the ultimate freedom.

"
It's like having a beachfront house at all of my favourite surf spots. A room with a view – who wouldn't want that?

For van lifer Mitch Williams, living out of a van means he gets to wake up, roll out of bed and find himself at some of his favourite beaches, including ones along the Great Ocean Road outside his hometown of Melbourne, Australia.

Cleaning up the coast

Natalie Woods had probably cleared hundreds of pieces of rubbish from beaches before. But the first piece of rubbish she remembers hauling off the sand was an old bread tray, washed up on a beach far from any bakery. She was searching for meaning at the time, looking for new ways of living outside of her 9-to-5 job. After picking up this one piece of plastic, Natalie started seeking out beaches strewn with rubbish – the sort avoided by regular beachgoers. She cleared one beach, then another and another, the stream of rubbish seemingly endless. Inspired, she co-founded the Clean Coast Collective – an organisation committed to cleaning up Australia's coastline – with her partner, Daniel Smith.

We never set out to start a beach cleanup organisation, or to clean beaches at all.

I'm not even sure why we picked up that first piece of rubbish – it can't have been the first we'd picked up on a beach, but it was the first that stuck in our minds. It was a brown plastic bread crate – the type you would see at your school canteen, piled high with fresh bread rolls. But this one was covered in barnacles and was on a beach. It had obviously been at sea for a while and, without thinking, we just picked it up and started dragging it back with us.

We were at a point in our lives where we were seeking something more fulfilling than our 9-to-5 lives. We were stuck in the daily grind, working Monday through to Friday, then escaping to the beach on the weekend. The same thing, week after week, until we found that one piece of rubbish.

From that point on we became strange people, driven to find dirty beaches and clean them up. It was like a treasure hunt: looking at maps of the coastline to see which beaches might be the most affected, observing the swell updates not for surf, but for the next southerly, which would bring more plastic ashore. Speaking to locals along the coast, who recalled tales of beaches covered in plastic. 'Oh yes,' they would say, 'some friends hiked there and they said it was covered in fishing buoys! It was around that headland, but I'm not sure exactly where …'

To those around us at the time, I'm sure it seemed like we'd lost our minds. Perhaps it even seemed like a noble pursuit, to be devoting so much time to the land and sea. But we got just as much out of it as the environment did. We had an excuse to explore further than we had before, seeking out new beaches and new stretches of coastline. In the beginning it took us to new beaches in our local area. Eventually it took us around Australia's entire coastline.

During our beach cleanups, wandering the sand for hours on end, we found ourselves drifting into almost meditative states. Sometimes we would wander together, chatting about this or that, but for the most part we would head off in different directions, letting the ebb and flow of the rubbish take us away on our own adventures. Our minds would drift from our daily checklists and soon be drawn into our present surroundings … 'doesn't the air smell salty today?', or 'how crunchy the sand feels beneath my toes', or 'I've never seen a sea urchin that colour before'.

"

The task of searching for rubbish pulled our minds into the present, distracting us from the 'real world', just for those few hours.

There was no reason to stress or angst over an email that had to be sent or a task that needed to be done. We were too far from our computers for that to matter. The task of searching for rubbish pulled our minds into the present, distracting us from the 'real world', just for those few hours.

At times we would cross paths with old salty seadogs: men who had lived and breathed that coastline for almost a century, who would gruffly mumble, 'You're wasting your time. You won't be able to clean up this mess'. We would just smile and continue on our way. Perhaps they had a point – perhaps the problem was too big for us to fix.

But … surely there's no harm in trying?
..........x

> "
> Sometimes we would wander together, chatting about this or that, but for the most part we would head off in different directions, letting the ebb and flow of the rubbish take us away on our own adventures.

When Ashley Hill started going on thru-hikes, she discovered a pastime that made her feel strong, grounded, challenged and at peace. Though she expected to feel lonely out on her own, she found that being alone made her more open to the joys of the trails she walked like the Te Araroa in New Zealand.

Finding the path

Ashley Hill had no hiking experience when she decided to walk the Pacific Crest Trail in North America. Her mum had recently died of cancer at the age of fifty-five, and Ashley needed space to grieve and room to grow. She knew she had to follow her dreams and live her life to the full, no matter how crazy it seemed. So she set off southbound, walking from Canada to Mexico on a solo trip that was meant to take six months. Three years later, Ashley is still hiking, still adventuring and still discovering herself along the way.

What is the Pacific Crest Trail (PCT) and what made you decide to walk it solo as your first adventure?

The PCT is a slice of perfection. It is roughly a 4265-kilometre (2560-mile) trail from Canada to Mexico that passes through Washington State, Oregon and California. The route traverses twenty-five national forests and seven national parks, from scorching deserts to snow-capped 4000-metre (13,123-foot) mountains. I hiked solo to help me process my mother's passing. I was looking for solitude and struggle, to grieve and grow. The idea of being alone in the wilderness just seemed so therapeutic.

How did you find the experience as a solo hiker?

It was everything I was looking for and so much more. It became my zen. I never feel alone when I'm out there; it connects me so much more to the world, nature, community. Ego dissolves and I feel like I become part of something. I rarely get scared, either. This surprised me, coming from the city and being such a social human in my old life. Sure, there are times when I wish that I could share the sunset or a spectacular view with a loved one, but I have my camera and have made friends with my shadow, so there you go.

You go by the name Bloody Mary on the trail. How did you come by it?

It's a tradition on American thru-hikes to be given a trail name for something silly you've done. Hikers often take the name up as a kind of new identity, forgoing their birth name entirely.

I used to suffer from a condition I like to call 'drunk feet', where I would fall on average three times a day. I was just so distracted by all the mountain beauty! So my legs were a bloody mess in the beginning. I was coming into my second

resupply town to load up on food, covered with duct tape bandages and dried blood stains of pride. I asked the staff at the diner if I could get a bloody mary, and they renamed me on the spot!

What made you decide to keep adventuring after coming off the PCT?

Thru-hiking changed my life. I discovered so much about myself, while realising how little I knew about the world around me. When I finished the PCT, I was in a perfect position to continue on; I had quit my job, moved out of my apartment, detached from all bills and most material possessions. I had discovered something that brought me immense peace and joy. I learnt that I was an incredibly capable being and had a new belief that I could do things I never considered possible before.

After tackling the PCT and the Pacific Northwest Trail, you made your way to New Zealand to walk the Te Araroa (TA). Can you describe that hike?

The TA is a 3000-kilometre (1864-mile) route that spans the length of the country's two main islands, from Cape Reinga in the north to Bluff in the south. It starts on the seemingly endless 90 Mile Beach, followed by a mountainous mud pit of extreme fun! You'll find yourself wading through rivers for days on end, then frolicking across hilly farmland with the sheep. There is an eight-day paddle down the Whanganui River and risky mountain passes that will have you wondering if you'll make it out alive. Then there's the fact that about thirty per cent of the route is on paved road, literally bisecting major cities and residential areas. I see the Te Araroa more as a journey across a country than a trail … a journey with unique challenges at every corner.

How did you find walking in the landscapes of New Zealand as opposed to North America?

Challenging! I love a challenge, so it was a wonderful experience, but trails in New Zealand are definitely more extreme than the more established routes in the United States. Switchbacks, where a trail zigzags back and forth up a mountain to make it easier to climb, don't seem to exist in New Zealand. You simply go straight up and over, giving us hikers some rock-hard, superhuman calves! And why worry about building a trail beside a river when you can just walk through it for hours on end? I will never forget the mud … mud up to my thighs at times.

But then, the TA is extremely well-marked, making navigation much easier than on other routes I've hiked. Plus, the route has a spectacular hut system that provides welcome refuge from the weather. You can experience four seasons in one day on the hike. Hypothermia and drowning are big killers in the back country, so these huts are a wonderful thing to have. I struggled with all the road walking, but, all in all, the Te Araroa was an amazing experience and I wouldn't change a thing.

You've talked about your love of cowboy camping. What is that?

Cowboy camping is my favourite discovery in the outdoor world. It's simply sleeping under the stars without a shelter overhead. It took me nearly a month to build up the courage to finally try it, but since that day, I only pitch a shelter under threat of rain or snow. I am in love with stargazing and have a bucket-list goal to spot a UFO. I'm also quite lazy, and this method reduces my setup and cleanup time to nearly nothing.

What are the most satisfying moments of a hike?

When you realise you've been smiling from ear to ear for ninety straight days. When you start to use the moon's cycle as a calendar. When you forget what you look like because it has been so long since you've encountered a mirror. When you can identify the flavour of water; I never knew that fresh spring water bursting out of a mountain has the best taste on Earth. When you start your day at three in the morning, headlamp lighting your way, just so you can walk into a sunrise. Oh, just about everything on a hike is satisfying!

How do you manage to keep your pack lightweight on thru-hikes?

Redefining necessity is the first step to going lightweight. When I pack for a trip, I start with what is essential to survive: shelter, sleeping system, water purification system, navigation system, clothing, first aid kit and a pack to carry it all in. Then I try to lighten each of these things. For example, I cut my toothbrush in half and cut off all tags, zipper handles and pockets from my clothes. I trim unnecessary straps from my pack and cut the borders off my maps to save weight. Then I try to get multiple uses out of my gear: dental floss and a needle double as a sewing repair kit; my tarp is also used as a rain poncho so I don't have to carry an extra jacket. For everything else, I ask myself if it is worth its weight. A stove is a luxury item. I can survive on cold food, but that won't be very enjoyable, so I carry one with pleasure. Soap and deodorant – nope, I'll take a shower when I get to town! X

" I discovered so much about myself, while realising how little I knew about the world around me.

"

I was looking for solitude and struggle, to grieve and grow. The idea of being alone in the wilderness just seemed so therapeutic.

The conviviality of a bonfire

Karri Hedge could mark the passing of time with her yearly bonfire. It always happened just as the season was tipping over into winter, before the bone-stripping chill descended. The invites were sent to family and friends, calling them out to the Australian country, where Karri and her family would have spent weeks forming a giant structure made of branches.

All sorts of friends gathered: those who were comfortable in the country and those who rarely left the city; groups and couples and families. Once the bonfire was lit, all barriers and pretensions fell away. New friends scrambled about, lobbing more kindling onto the fire, and old friends chatted and burned mementos, drunk on wine and the entrancing power of the flames.

The invitation always said they should wear their warmest clothes. But every year, I worried that someone wouldn't understand just how cold it gets out here. So we gathered old coats and hats and scarves into a pile, just in case.

The week before the bonfire, I'd become an obsessive weather-checker. Seven days out, the rain would be predicted to be torrential, the winds gale-force, and I would despair. Six days out, the storm would have moved forward a day and we were going to be okay! Five days out, the gloom would descend again. Three days out, you could generally rely on the forecast, but it didn't stop me praying for a late game-changing miracle.

I don't know why I worried about the weather, year on year. The party happened regardless. Sometimes we huddled inside around the stove, hiding from the rain, and sometimes we sat outside, marvelling at the crystal-clear sky sprayed with stars.

" There is something intimate and exhilarating about a fire in the darkness.

When the time came, rain or not, we always made our way along a lantern-lit path to the towering pile of branches at the back of the property.

My dad would call the local fire brigade the afternoon before to notify them about the fire – the responsible thing to do. 'That's right, two cubic metres', he'd say, with a wink to me. It was more like twenty.

Friends who were there for the first time would make their way with old timers through the unknown darkness until they were told to stop. They had no concept, yet, of how high the stacked branches towered above them – where the pile began or ended.

The newspaper and firelighters, tucked into nooks and crannies by the light of a phone, would be lit. They flared promisingly, and we whooped and cheered. Yet these fires always burnt themselves out, leaving nothing but a few twigs glowing in the darkness.

Dad would go and get the kerosene. It never worked, but he always went to get it anyway and sprayed it liberally, splashing it over gumboots and into mugs of wine. It made a satisfying *WHUMPH* when it was lit, and then, predictably, it fizzled out. Every time.

Tactics were discussed. A better, drier spot found amidst the pile and the lighting process repeated: newspaper, firelighters, matches. On the other side of the pile, a rival team's fledgling fire would crackle into view, spurring us on. We tended our new fire, feeding it lovingly with dry twigs and leaves.

Some people were content to watch. Some were directors, arguing about the dampness of the wood or the direction of the wind. Then there were the doers. They brought headlamps so they could find the driest kindling at the bottom of the bonfire, and climbed right into the pile to reach it. They worked tirelessly, feeding ever-greedier flames until they became self-sustaining.

The flames would take hold, climbing quickly, lighting up the surrounding faces with an orange glow. The ring of watchers retreated gradually, all turning like lambs on a spit, as they warmed themselves in the fierce heat.

There is something intimate and exhilarating about a fire in the darkness. Couples huddle together, watching the flames – eyes shining, arms intertwined. Children dart in and out of the surrounding trees, revelling in the intermittent freedom from adult eyes. The more daring ones poke at the flames with long sticks, giggling at the shower of sparks they send flying into the air. A roar of solidarity might ring out as someone throws a symbol of a troubled past into the fire: a ritual sacrifice for a new beginning.

As the fire dwindled, people would dribble back towards the house to refill drinks or put the kids to bed. Eventually everyone followed, drunk on fire and wine. There were games and songs into the early hours.

In the morning, we'd walk back to the bonfire site. 'The walk seemed so much longer in the dark!' someone would say. We would round the corner to see a circle of ash, still smoking gently.

As people left, they might pass my dad in the driveway with the chainsaw out. He'd wave them off and return to his sawing. Already working on next year's bonfire.

..........X

❝

A roar of solidarity might ring out as someone throws a symbol of a troubled past into the fire: a ritual sacrifice for a new beginning.

Every year, Karri Hedge and her family would invite their friends to gather around a bonfire on their property. Sometimes they would throw old mementos into the flames – symbols of a troubled past, burned with hope for a new beginning.

Riding through hardship and on to joy

When Dan Marsh started dreaming of going on a solo bike journey, he initially planned to ride from Melbourne, Victoria to Lake Eyre, South Australia – a journey of more than 1000 kilometres (620 miles) into Australia's harsh desert centre – to photograph the sun-cracked salt plains of the usually dry lake. But after months of dreaming and planning, he thought to himself: why stop at Lake Eyre?

Dan left Melbourne with everything he'd need strapped to the back of his bike. He headed south along the surfers' coastal route towards Adelaide, then left the beach behind to ride up through the centre of Australia and, eventually, across to Queensland's tropical north. It was six months of adventure, a solo ride characterised by the generosity of the people he met along the way and the grandeur of the landscapes he passed through.

I daydreamed for three years about riding my bike alone through Australia, along the coast and up through the Red Centre. I wanted to travel without time constraints, just camping, surfing, connecting with people, shooting photos and living a footloose existence.

Whenever I told anyone my plans, they'd give me a weird look or say that it didn't really sound like much of a holiday. But I loved camping and riding, and I was obsessed with the idea of this adventure.

It wasn't until a few weeks before I left that I actually started to have fears; before that, I'd romanticised about the adventure rather than actually thinking about what I was getting myself into.

> **I realised I was holding on to the struggles – and I just had to let everything go.**

The day I rode out of Melbourne, it hit me like a tonne of bricks: everything I'd dreamed about for so long was happening, and it scared the shit out of me. It was overwhelming and surreal riding off with no real thought of when I'd be back, leaving behind a lover and everything else to chase some kind of fantasy, loaded up on a bike so heavy that I could hardly ride it down the street let alone halfway around Australia. What was I thinking?

I definitely wasn't fit or prepared for the experience, but I don't think that I could ever have really prepared my body or mind for what I was about to put it through. I really struggled in the first couple of weeks; my body hurt, the riding was tough, and sleeping on the hard ground in my freezing tent took its toll on me.

But then something kind of clicked. I realised I was holding on to the struggles – and I just had to let everything go. After that pivotal moment, everything became easier. My mind relaxed and all the relentless chatter about how hard everything was seemed to fall away. I became more present with every kilometre, and each day was a joy.

It was funny – once I'd gotten into the rhythm of my new life, it became my everyday reality. From the outside it seemed crazy and wild, but to me it was just … my life. I was entrenched in it, loving every single day. I felt a beautiful sense of freedom that I'd never really experienced before. I was often alone in isolated places, but I never felt lonely; just to sit by myself out in the wild was a special experience.

And I met so many people on the road who helped me out in some way, with beds, meals, showers and rides. Their outright generosity was so heartwarming.

As much as riding thousands of kilometres was about riding a bike and pushing my physical limits, it was also about so much more than that. The road taught me so much about myself, and life in general. I was content living in the dirt, smelly and filthy a lot of the time, but not really caring. Being limited to only what I could carry, I discovered that I loved the simplicity of having very little. Fears come and go, but they're only fears; they're not facts. I learnt that once I pushed past them, anything was possible.

I'm stoked with what I was able to achieve, particularly with the support of my partner, who understood my dreams and desires. When I finally made it to Far North Queensland, she took up the challenge and joined me on the road. We rode down the east coast together, planning to end up in Melbourne … but we made it as far as Byron Bay, New South Wales, and haven't quite left. One day we'll finish the journey. But life's pretty good where we are right now.

··········X

> **"**
> Fears come and go, but they're only fears; they're not facts. I learnt that once I pushed past them, anything was possible.

> **"**
> It was funny – once I'd gotten into the rhythm of my new life, it became my everyday reality. From the outside it seemed crazy and wild, but to me it was just ... my life.

A land of ice and fire

As we approached what looked like a former Soviet-period state collective farm, we saw an old Russian Mi-8 helicopter being fuelled and a couple of men tinkering with its engine. The sight of people fussing with the engine of the helicopter in which we were about to fly didn't exactly soothe our nerves. It looked run down, its back doors held closed with a length of string. A tentative-looking way to get to the heart of a rugged, untamed land.

We'd only recently arrived in Petropavlovsk-Kamchatsky, the capital (and only) city in the Kamchatka region of the Russian Federation. Kamchatka is a large peninsula in far-eastern Russia, on the Pacific Ocean north of Japan. An area of some 270,000 square kilometres (about 100,000 square miles), it is sparsely populated. It holds some 300,000 people, most of whom live in Petropavlovsk-Kamchatsky. Beyond the city is a dramatic land – a living place of geysers, glaciers and wild weather, along with 160 volcanoes, sixteen of which are still active.

> ❝
> We felt insignificant in the face of a vast horizon full of mountains and volcanoes; a landscape devoid of human habitation. This, we realised, was how Earth once was.

The helicopter was taking us to Kurilskoye Lake on the southern part of the Kamchatka Peninsula, where wildness and isolation reigned. After swallowing our apprehension, we were ushered on board, our luggage stacked in the middle as we sat around on side seats, military-style.

The helicopter flew low, keeping out of the higher altitude winds and staying close to the tundra. We opened some of the windows and saw a vast green land outstretched below us, intersected by streams and with no signs of human life. The horizon was pierced by multiple cones, their tops in the clouds – volcanoes. It had the air of a lost world.

A bit over an hour later, we were dropped off at Kurilskoye Lake. We settled into a newly built, large cabin surrounded by wire fences to keep the local bear population out. The lake is a nature park reserve, and we were there as the guests of two resident rangers. The rangers would get snowed in during winter, but it was late August – the peak of summer – and the temperatures were humid and mild.

The next day we moved north to the nearest volcano, travelling in a six-wheel-drive converted military truck across riverbeds, climbing as far as the truck could take us. Continuing on foot, we trekked the long approach across rising ground and snowfields. The terrain became steeper closer to the top of the volcano. We encountered vents of steam and sulphur, reminding us that the volcano was only slumbering.

When we finally reached the top, we were surrounded by a landscape of ice and fire – a place where the Earth showed its power to change and control its landscapes. We felt insignificant in the face of a vast horizon full of mountains and volcanoes; a landscape devoid of human habitation. This, we realised, was how Earth once was. We felt fortunate to witness it.

..........x

Words by Stephanie and Doron Francis. Images and captions by Alexander Gerasimov, who loves to explore Russia's wild spaces.

The first time I visited Kamchatka it was winter, when the weather is severe and there are no tourists. Upon arrival, I took my tent and went to the shore of the Pacific Ocean. It was there I first met the winter surfers, who surf even when the water is 2°C (36°F), chasing the beauty of a sea surrounded by snow. I stood on the shore, drawn into the meditation of the surfers, the cold and the landscape.

Kamchatka is very far away from Moscow, where I was raised; thousands of kilometres to the east. I dreamed of this primeval place on the shores of the Pacific Ocean, with its volcanoes, geysers and mountains, almost untouched by man. It's a crazy place. Here you can climb to a volcano's crater and surf in the cold ocean, or see a bear or wolverine in its natural habitat.

Life on the lake

They say life is just about long enough to get good at one thing, so you should choose it wisely. Up until his late twenties, Padraig Croke's sole focus was his career as a graphic designer, but a New Year's resolution to spend more time outdoors led him from the bustling city life of Dublin, Ireland, to Sweden's serene Lake Immeln. He knew he needed to change his focus, but the shift from his old life was not instant; it was gradual and purposeful. His passion for creating went from design to bushcraft, and the desire to capture that journey overtook almost everything else.

The lake of Immeln, in the south of Sweden, covers about 22 square kilometres (9 square miles) and holds over two hundred islands in its crystal-clear waters. It is my home, and I use every spare moment I have exploring its shores and forests. I spent my thirty-first birthday alone out here on a warm June night, perfectly content with just sitting by the fire – I even took a naked midnight dip to celebrate! I have awoken on October mornings to chilly winter winds whispering the turn of the seasons through my tent door, the wild waves on the lake daring me to paddle my canoe home. I have sat with my girlfriend on a remote island, drinking beers and watching the sun set to the west. It would take a person many years to know this lake intimately, but I'm in no rush.

> **I have awoken on October mornings to chilly winter winds whispering the turn of the seasons through my tent door, the wild waves on the lake daring me to paddle my canoe home.**

The lake and the forest surrounding it have become a vehicle for me to drive my creative needs. As a photographer I feel most at home when I am floating through this landscape, attempting in some way to capture exactly what it is I am experiencing. I love to document, be that through photography, writing, or sometimes with film. I often worry if this overwhelming urge to capture something actually takes me out of the moment. But mostly, I think, I feel centred when I'm out there. People say their hobbies can be an escape from their daily lives. When they are focused on their craft, nothing else is on their mind. I am lucky enough to have found a way to make my hobby and my passion a lifestyle. But I have not always been here, and only a few years ago my life was very different.

I am from Dublin, Ireland – a far cry from the wilderness that now sits on my doorstep. Today my love for the outdoors is fierce, but in my early twenties I was following a very different trajectory. My future was about earning good money so I could own a house near the city, close to the bars and restaurants, the buzz and the bustle. I spent five years studying graphic design and another seven in various studios, working my way up the ranks.

A whimsical New Year's resolution to get outside more on the weekends found me looking for Facebook groups to get involved with. Ironically, the wonders of the internet allowed me to stumble upon online communities of folks getting back to nature and focusing on bushcraft skills, rather than the latest high-tech hiking equipment. Terms like 'wilderness skills' and 'bushcraft' were entirely unknown to me then. I knew what camping was, of course. I had spent nights in the back garden in a tent with my buddies, maybe even a forest once or twice. But as a lifestyle? To learn how to chop wood, to use tools and build a camp from scratch was something I had never even considered. I was hooked!

My new circle of like-minded friends eventually led me here to Sweden, on a group canoe trip on Lake Immeln, and I fell in love almost instantly. I knew I had to find a way to stay. Luckily for me, the man who owned the canoes we rented, now my boss, was happy to take me on. 'There's a small cabin down by the water you can have, if you want it? You can work for your rent.' Of course I wanted it, and after some logistical shifting and deliberating, I quit my job in Ireland and moved to Lake Immeln.

I still love design though, and I have a small client base that keeps me ticking over. On workdays I'm in the canoe centre, helping customers and managing our website. On my days off I go camping. The pace of my life has slowed – I even find myself walking slower, after years of city life having turned me into a power walker.

Life here is not without its compromises: in the low season it is quiet – sometimes unbearably so – my living situation is simple and my transport options somewhat limited. But when I am out on the lake or walking through the forest, I am simultaneously focused and carefree. My camera is by my side, my pack is on my back and I am altogether content with my lot.

..........X

> "
> When I am out on the lake or walking through the forest, I am simultaneously focused and carefree.

A home made by hand

Shane Hurt and Queenie Yehenala trucked a shipping container onto a 20-hectare (50-acre) property near the town of Kinglake in Victoria, Australia, hiding it deep in the woods. The two designers, who met in Shanghai years before, turned this shipping container into a vacation home, built of plywood and paint. It was a chance to use their hands, disconnect from the city and share a connection with family and friends.

You'll need to drive down a bumpy, steep gravel road, and then an even bumpier dirt road, to get to Shane and Queenie's home in the thick forest near Kinglake. There are few remaining tall gum trees here, their trunks black and cracked as a reminder of the fire that tore through this land ten years ago, taking lives, houses and communities. The rest of the trees are striplings, light and skinny, sticking their trunks out with bravado as they reach for the sky.

It was fire that took the original house on the property, a mid-century modern structure with clear views down to the river that is now obscured by upstart gums.

Shane and Queenie's house, placed in a clearing halfway up the hill, is a 6-metre (20-foot) shipping container. They trucked it onto the property as an iron shell, the old company logo still printed on its side.

The container both contrasts and is at home with its surroundings; it's made noticeable by the deck around it and the tools strewn on the ground outside. Over time, Shane and Queenie have turned this shell into a home, complete with kitchen, reading nook, a single bed and a queen bed loft. The interior is simple and striking, befitting its size, with exposed pale wood and black details.

They come here to unplug, to unwind as a family: lighting candles, cooking on a barbecue, washing up in a bucket and slapping away the mosquitoes that slip in through the doors. It's more like camping than a traditional holiday home. The family relax out on the deck, swaying in the hammock, after days spent making a home in the bush.

..........X

"

They come here to unplug, to unwind as a family: lighting candles, cooking on a barbecue, washing up in a bucket and slapping away the mosquitoes that slip in through the doors.

Shane Hurt and Queenie Yehenala wanted a weekend cottage to call their own – something that harmonised with nature rather than something that fought against it. They made it out of a shipping container, creating a peaceful place to unwind.

Night vision

By day, Kate Armstrong's summer camp was a busy, known world. But that world changed overnight, when a group of campers and their counsellors spent the night in the woods after everyone else had gone home. Night transformed their woods from known to unknown, the campers from comfortable to hovering on the edge of fear. But after the campfire was doused and sleeping bags were rolled out, they'd go on a night walk. The rules were simple: no flashlights, no voices. Just sneakers and feet, ears and eyes laid open to the dark.

We would gather along the side of the gymnastics hut. It was just a roof, four pillars and a platform, open on all sides to miles of woods. The campers would inch in close around us counsellors, eyes made huge by the thrill of being the only ones left.

By day, our camp was endlessly loud – filled with the splash and crash of water games and arrows thwacking targets; the rise and fall of singalongs and names being shouted between the trees. These girls were the queens of that daytime kingdom. At twelve, they were the oldest, confident in every step of the path.

"
No one's immune to a fear of the dark. It's built into our bodies, ancient and bone-deep.

But camp was different after the buses left and the sun sank down below the treeline. Night turned our knowable, well-worn woods into something strange and, if we were honest, a little scary. The paths became pale lines swallowed by things we couldn't see.

No one's immune to a fear of the dark. It's built into our bodies, ancient and bone-deep. We fill the darkness with our scariest monsters and every troubling thought we ignore when it's light. That's why our ancestors learnt to light fires and tell stories around them. They wanted to control the darkness – to push it back and out of reach.

The gym had no electric lights – just our flashlights. Without those, the only light came from the moon and, if you squinted, the lichen that glowed around the base of certain tree trunks. These campers were city kids, used to quick and easy ways of dispelling darkness. They had never known a room free of phone glow and street lamp, or the light that creeps in around a slightly cracked door.

Inevitably, one of the campers would ask: *how will we see without flashlights?*

And we would tell them: *you've got to let your eyes adjust.*

Close your eyes, nice and tight. Keep them closed and count to ten. When you open them, don't let them settle on any one thing. Just let them wander and your night vision will come.

When we first opened our eyes, there were just vague shapes and shadows. But then details would start to emerge: the deep grooves carved into the tree trunks; the edges of the pebbles that littered the trail; the bright corners of someone's teeth as they smiled. The stars were brighter, now. Their outlines flickered in our eyes like tiny fires.

We would line up, everyone within an arm's length of each other. One counsellor would walk in front, one in back – the braver job. It was hard to shake that eyes-on-the-back-of-your-neck feeling. Even knowing we weren't in danger, the dark made our senses hard to trust.

No one was allowed to talk, a rule almost as important as the one about flashlights. Light and sound both do the same job: they wrap you up in a self-made universe, blocking out the rest of the world. But we wanted to help our campers strip away that buffer. To show them what happens when you let the darkness in.

In the beginning, the silence was always too much for them. We could feel how badly they wanted to fill it – a familiar laugh or cough to make the darkness feel less like a living thing. But then they would start to hear their footsteps, soft against the dirt of the path. Their heads would tilt towards leaves as they shivered, and towards squirrels overturning the underbrush. The woods would come alive around them, but it didn't feel threatening. It felt more like a secret being shared.

After a while we no longer had to *shhhhh* them. They were too awed by the silence to want to break it apart.

We wound downhill through oaks and poplars. Eventually, we would get down to the lake. The campers would sit along the wooden bridge that led to the kayak shed, looking out over the water and the trees beyond. The longer we sat, the more we noticed: the reflections of the stars on the water and the skating insects that broke them. The chorus of bullfrogs, so haunting and deep. Our breaths blended in, becoming a part of the forest's cadence. Making space for us in this place we all loved.

The darkness became an invitation: to stop, to listen, to feel the parts of these woods we couldn't access when everything was loud and bright. There was nothing to fear, if we embraced it.

We just had to let our eyes adjust.

..........X

> ❝
> The darkness became an invitation: to stop, to listen, to feel the parts of these woods we couldn't access when everything was loud and bright.

Carving out a good life

Charlie Gladstone has made a career out of pioneering a new kind of living. Born to a famous name (his great-great grandfather was William Ewart Gladstone, a former prime minister of Great Britain) and heir to two grand properties, he and his wife, Caroline, chose to move away from London and raise their children in the wilds of Scotland. It was there they founded online shop Pedlars, which champions artisan products from around the British Isles.

The Good Life Experience, co-founded with Cerys Matthews and Steve Abbott, is their latest adventure – an annual festival in Wales that's about reconnecting with nature and a community of like-minded people who build things that last, whether that's a relationship, a craft or a meditative practice.

What is The Good Life Experience?

It's a unique celebration of what goes into living 'the good life'. It asks a complex question and tries to simplify it: what do I really want from life? Our answers are presented to our guests over two-and-a-half days each September, and they are: family; amazing food; great music; the ability to learn new crafts and meet new friends; dogs; fascinating talks; engagement with outdoor activities; campfires; nights under canvas; extreme friendliness and politeness; no litter; and the coming together of like-minded people.

What inspired you to start the festival?

I always wanted to do a festival. I was toying with notions of the good life after the global financial meltdown, trying to figure out what it was that people really, truly wanted from their lives. I was asking myself this both because I am a businessman and because I am genuinely interested in the intellectual side of things. I have children, and I wondered if my children really wanted a world of cheap goods, endless shopping, gold-plated restaurants, clothes they could throw away after five wears, endless screen time, food flown to their table from Africa, no spare time. My conclusion was that while these things were perhaps okay in small measures, I wanted them to buy things they treasured and that would last, to know how these things were made, to climb trees and throw axes and discover new ways of looking at the world.

Because I am equal parts brave and reckless, I figured that we might be able to make a festival that celebrates all of this. And because we have a lovely farm in Wales and lots of interesting friends whom we thought might like to perform and suggest people to perform – not to mention two brilliant friends in our co-founders – we gave it a go.

The festival puts a lot of emphasis on connecting with the outdoors and reconnecting with old crafts. Why do you think it's important for people to get outside and use their hands?

I am fundamentally an outdoors person. We raised our six children in the Scottish Highlands, in a remote location, as a conscious choice. We even wrote a book on it, called *The Family Guide to the Great Outdoors*. Everyone should get outside and exhaust themselves from time to time. If all young people got to climb a tree and throw an axe and run up a hill once or twice a week, there would be no fighting in the street. The need to make things with your hands is as old – or older than – the hills. We all have it in us, but mass consumerism has handed it to foreign factories where labour is cheap. But ever since the financial crash in 2008, some people have been thinking about how what they consume is made and what that means, from food to jeans to tableware. These are our people.

"

Everyone should
get outside
and exhaust
themselves from
time to time.

What does the good life mean to the festival founders?

Well, the festival means massive amounts of work, arguments, stress and – simultaneously – fun, pride, creativity, the adrenaline of risk. For me, the good life is all the things we offer at the festival: family, friends both new and old – we have met masses of brilliant new people through the event – music, being outdoors, shenanigans, proper food …

I think of the festival like this: the day is for learning, meeting people, listening, thinking, discovering things, trying new skills and running around; the night is for going a bit bonkers with a great cocktail in your hand and some amazing music.

One of the most popular events at the festival is axe-throwing, which is a very niche skill. What about throwing an axe do you think gives people enjoyment?

The axe is the oldest tool known to humankind. We all have a connection to it, whether we know it or not. And when we hold it and throw it and it hits the target … BOOM!

Do you think people see the festival as a momentary escape from modern life, or more as something they can take home with them?

It's a bit of both. They can come and learn stuff and take those skills home. They can come and have fun and have a monumental hangover on Monday, but feel that they had a life-enhancing experience.

..........X

66

If all young people got to climb a tree and throw an axe and run up a hill once or twice a week, there would be no fighting in the street.

X

The Good Life Festival, held in Wales once a year, is a celebration of life's simple pleasures: stimulating conversation, good music, learning new skills and spending ample amounts of time outside, climbing trees and using your hands.

"

If there's no next adventure on your mind, then what you're working towards might not be worth the investment.

Choose adventure over email

It can be tempting to forget to look around, captive as we are to the screens in front of us. For Graham Hiemstra, it's the call of adventure that keeps him looking away from his screen in New York City – whether that's hiking the romantically named Rainbow Mountain in Peru or a weekend surf down the coast. He founded The Field, an online adventure repository that entices its readers, through good design and good stories, to look around, to see what's out there, to book that next trip. After all, if you're not exploring ... what's the point of it all?

We'd only been on the trail a short while that morning, but our legs still held the memory of miles covered over previous days as we trekked deep into the Peruvian Andes – and let's not even mention the altitude. The four of us crouched down in a semicircle, trying to catch our breaths. With Mount Salkantay looming 6271 metres (20,574 feet) overhead, our Quechua guide performed a healing ceremony. Together, we made cocoa leaf offerings to the spirit protector of the Sacred Valley, who resides in the imposing mountain for which he's named. Like countless others who came before us, as far back as the Inca Empire, we gave thanks and wished each other luck with adventures yet to come. Then we ate some candy bars and starting walking, putting one foot in front of the other.

I grew up in the north-west corner of the United States, where exploring nature was something everyone did. Winters were spent skiing. In summer, my father and I would sleep on the porch under the stars more nights than not. If there was one rule, it was to never waste a clear day inside. I never considered living any other way. Hell, I never even considered living *that* way. It was just how it was. It wasn't until I left that I realised just how influential that early, easy access to adventure was.

These days New York City is home, a third of my time on this rock is gone, and it takes quite a bit more effort to really get outside. Though life in New York isn't easy, it is fun. And surprisingly rewarding, if you're willing to put the work in. At least that's what nearly nine million of us tell ourselves each morning as we cram into subway cars like sardines. But I've come to understand that, for me, the only way to truly thrive here is to leave at every opportunity I get.

Whether it's heading upstate for a weekend of camping, visiting the old growth forests and iconic peaks of America's west coast, or getting truly off the grid in a foreign country, going somewhere new will never get old. Travelling encourages you to expand your worldview and consider alternative perspectives. Nothing puts life's priorities back in place quite like willingly eating mushy food out of a vacuum-packed meal pouch and shitting in a dirt hole you dug yourself. Or, if you prefer a prettier picture, standing atop a 5000-metre (16,400-foot) pass, communing with a mountain spirit.

As a New Yorker, these experiences remind me how unimportant those ever-so-important emails actually are. And that nature is something I need – not a trend or a fad, even if it may feel like that at times.

Regardless of how far-flung or rudimentary the escape, the important thing is to keep them coming. Like all things worth holding on to in life, we require regular maintenance, both mentally and physically, and Mother Nature is the ultimate mechanic. You need to always have an answer to the question 'what's next?' If there's no next adventure on your mind, then what you're working towards might not be worth the investment.

..........x

> "
> Regardless of how far flung or rudimentary the escape, the important thing is to keep them coming.

When Graham Hiemstra headed off into the Peruvian Andes, he knew he would be up for some serious altitude and difficult days. But that was part of what made it a worthy adventure: nothing quite puts life into perspective like having to go it tough for a while.

The nature of Japan

With the bright lights and billboards of central Tokyo, Japan, as a backdrop for their everyday lives, Japanese-Australian couple Ippei and Janine Naoi place importance on creating a balance between living with modern conveniences and appreciating nature in its purest forms.

Janine, originally from Melbourne, Australia, comes from an outdoorsy family and regularly went on summer camping trips, where she discovered her love of the outdoors. Ippei, inspired by his father, who was a successful climber, also often went camping with friends and relatives as a child.

After meeting in Amsterdam in 2004, Ippei and Janine built their life together in Tokyo and now run two businesses: a jewellery design and production company with both retail and online stores, and a cinematic lifestyle photography business specialising in personal portraits and advertising images for global brands. Both enterprises allow Ippei and Janine to blend their creativity and love of outdoor adventure, with images of nature often appearing throughout their collections. The couple are also ambassadors for Sony Xperia smartphones, which increases their scope for connecting with people through their photography. This link is one of their main inspirations. 'We want to capture the story of the places we visit and portray images of positivity to inspire optimism and motivate more people to explore the beautiful, natural environment that surrounds them.'

Self-described 'wild campers', Ippei and Janine rarely stay at authorised campsites, unless it's a requirement of the national park they visit. Their typical adventures involve hiking, fishing, and packrafting in secluded areas around Japan only accessible by kayak. Before they invested in their own packraft, the couple say, 'We'd been camping and seen beautiful, secluded beaches and wondered how to access them.' Experiences on several kayak tours also opened their eyes to the potential of packrafting and the places it could take them. Some of the couple's favourite areas to explore include Iriomote Island and Ishigaki, a part of the Yaeyama Island group in Okinawa, which Janine describes as 'a slice of paradise'; and Nagatoro River, which flows through the prefectures of Saitama and Tokyo and evokes a countryside feeling. 'It's like a breath of fresh air within easy reach of the city,' says Janine.

> **"**
>
> We want to capture the story of the places we visit and portray images of positivity to inspire optimism and motivate more people to explore the beautiful, natural environment that surrounds them.

> "
> The concept of satoyama ... refers to places where human beings and nature coexist in symbiotic relationships.

As for Ippei, he believes Japanese people have a unique connection to nature. Not only does Japan have the third-highest forest cover rate among developed nations – about 70 per cent of land nationwide – but densely forested mountains are a common sight, with many people perceiving mountains to be sacred places. The concept of satoyama, a Japanese word that refers to places where human beings and nature coexist in symbiotic relationships, is another way Ippei interprets Japan's harmony with nature. In satoyama culture, 'humans are a part of the ecosystem', Ippei explains, and although there is natural diversity in different regions, co-dependence between humans and nature is a permanent fixture. In this approach to biodiversity, people often gather food for animals from grasslands and collect firewood from only the surrounding areas.

However, Ippei feels there is a sense that Japanese people who live rurally sometimes lack appreciation of their natural surroundings, as is evident through indecorous rubbish dumping and the commercial development of secluded, previously untouched beaches. He has also observed that inner-city residents tend to prioritise modern convenience and anonymity over exploring nature. After working long hours amid the city's bustle, they prefer to fade into the crowd rather than feel more conspicuous in an open natural setting. As well as this, Ippei remarks that 'due to the vast number of natural disasters Japan experiences each year, people are cautious of the risks associated with being adventurous in the outdoors and the true force of nature.'

The philosophy Ippei and Janine follow is simple: reside in a city where established infrastructure can be maximised while nature is left intact. In doing this, Janine hopes they can instil the same values in their daughter. 'We want to teach her to appreciate everyday life in the city as well as provide opportunities for her to live without convenience and appreciate and respect the wilderness.' At the same time, Ippei and Janine are aware of the potential environmental costs of overtourism. 'If everyone did this type of travel, it wouldn't be sustainable. Without proper knowledge and experience, secluded places could become overcrowded and misused.' As for the future, Ippei and Janine hope to provide more visual strength to brands that align with their lifestyle. 'We want to continue exploring new places, having epic adventures, and creating more challenges and different perspectives for our daughter through a connection with the outdoors.'

..........x

Words by Nyree Jacobs, university lecturer, urban nature-lover and long-term resident of Japan. Images and captions by Ippei and Janine Photography (Ippei and Janine Naoi).

This photo was taken by Janine and Ippei during a packrafting trip in the Yanbaru National Park on Okinawa Main Island. Tree ferns grow in abundance in this dense subtropical rainforest, which is also home to many endemic species. It is often raining which creates a magical atmosphere when the humidity mixes with the warm air. As the rain came down, we took shelter under umbrella-like tree ferns by the banks of the lake, where in wonder, our daughter immediately started asking us about the possibility of spotting a dinosaur!

The meaning of travel

Matty Hannon quit his job working in advertising to ride a motorcycle from Alaska to Argentina, surfing the waves and the road all 13,500 kilometres (8500 miles) down the long trans-American coastline. He didn't go in pursuit of that life-changing moment, that picture-perfect revelation, but instead with the plan to find and document inspiring people across America with his camera. It was a trip characterised by curiosity and a deep appreciation for the people and lands he met along the way. This curiosity led to a chance encounter with a girl named Heather, who ended up joining Matty on the road.

Leaving home is an exhilarating prospect: the allure of an open road, the promise of rolling waves, of neatly groomed ski hills with perfect fireside retreats. It's easy to let your imagination run wild at the sight of the magazines in the supermarket's travel section, while your tired fingers grip the sticky handles of your coffee-laden shopping trolley.

You gaze at the glossy covers. How good would life be if you could just make *that* your next destination? Make those smiling people your friends? Have just one of those '15 Vacations That Will Change Your Life'?

But beyond the allure of a few weeks off work, some stimulating views, a peer-approved tan and extra fodder for your Instagram – is all this travel really growing you? Is it benefiting us? Is it promoting understanding and tolerance, or just fostering elitism and homogeny? Are we learning from the places we visit, or are we imposing ourselves on places that would be better off without us? Aren't we supposed to be using less energy, staying local, buying local? And why aren't we returning from these 'life-changing' destinations with … different lives?

Perhaps because like most marketing, social media and all things shiny, it lacks a little soul or deeper meaning – travel, for many, has become just another commodity. But the real essence of travel is still there for discovery … it just helps to have a meaningful reason to go.

In my own travels, I chose to make film my medium, surfing my canvas, and time my currency. I quit my job in Australia and embarked on a trans-continental motorcycle and surfing journey from Alaska to Argentinean Patagonia. I aimed to find and interview inspiring people across the Americas, to document their ideas. One of the first sequences I filmed was an urban farm in British Columbia, where I interviewed

> " Travel, for many, has become just another commodity. But the real essence of travel is still there for discovery … it just helps to have a meaningful reason to go.

its owner. That cute entrepreneur ended up joining me on my journey to South America. Heather and I have been together ever since.

We rode south, interviewing fifty people across North and South America. It was in those deep conversations that I found meaning in the idea of 'travel' or 'adventure', immersing myself in diverse opinions, reflecting and making adjustments in the way I chose to live. Our interviews with farmers living in a traditional farming community in the Andes, who inspired us to sell our motorcycles and continue our journey on horseback.

It's at such times that I find documentary filmmaking a beautiful process. By offering someone a microphone and a willing ear, you're offering them the chance to be heard. And in contrast to the surface conversations that define most people's days, you can ask deep and probing questions and be met with honest, sometimes profound, responses that have the power to rattle even your core beliefs.

But just like you don't need a glossy magazine travel holiday – not really – most people don't need a documentary camera and a microphone to experience the world. The only true necessity is deep appreciation and curiosity. Perhaps we need that now more than ever.

That alone behoves us to travel – just where and how *well* we travel is up to us.

..........X

"

... most people don't need a documentary camera and a microphone to experience the world. The only true necessity is deep appreciation and curiosity.

When Matty Hannon hit the road on his motorcycle, heading south from Alaska towards Argentina, he didn't expect some of what he found along the way: fascinating people to interview, new ways of thinking and a girl with whom to fall in love and sleep under stars in the Atacama Desert.

" ... I found meaning
in the idea of 'travel'
or 'adventure',
immersing myself
in diverse opinions,
reflecting and making
adjustments in the way
I chose to live.

Capturing the beauty of a damaged world

Brooke Holm became a photographer almost by accident. She was working in an advertising agency when someone put a camera in her hand and told her to go take photos of some outdoor billboards the company had produced. She took the photos, everyone was pleased, and Brooke was hooked, so much so that she went back to school to develop her skills. Brooke has become a sought-after commercial photographer in Australia and the United States, but it's her work photographing nature – the human-made and human-affected places of the world – that truly speak to and for her. They showcase her passion for the environment and for highlighting places many of us don't get to see.

You mix a commercial practice with your own artistic work. How do you balance the two?

While my commercial work is driven by living and working in a big city amongst the craziness, my personal, artistic work is the complete opposite. It's my escape and my chance to shoot exactly what I want. There is no brief or client to please – it's all about what is important to me. Currently, this work is exploring a deeper understanding of the world in a social and environmental sense.

My art has always been driven by landscapes, and humans' relationships to nature, particularly mine. However, these days I feel there are deeper avenues to explore – ones that might not be pleasant, but that contain vital stories and important questions.

How important is nature to your work?

Nature is the most important aspect of my work. My practice is centred around the environment and our relationship with it. Nature and humans affect each other in many ways, so there should be a mutual give and take. Instead it seems one-sided, where we take and hardly give anything back. I'm constantly wrestling with ideas about how to convey the importance of respecting and nurturing our planet. Our dependency on its resources has become such a big burden, in a very unsustainable way.

Everything in this world is connected. That reality becomes more alarming as our seas become more acidic and species die out, which is leading to some devastating consequences – all because of us. We can't fight a volcano with weapons, and we definitely can't buy a new Great Barrier Reef once we eventually destroy it.

What does nature mean to you personally?

It's the only thing that really makes perfect sense to me. I don't know for sure, but I feel it's partly based on a primal instinct where the connection is naturally strong and unexplainable.

When I see all the terrible things affecting our environment, it really disturbs me. There is a deep desire in me for exploration and discovery, for finding new perspectives on places in both a physical and mental sense. Nature finds a way to make you question what really matters. Finding these landscapes and documenting them is a very personal thing, but I feel a responsibility to share my findings with people, as many are not fortunate enough to leave their hometown or do not remember how to look outside their comfort zone. I like to inspire deeper thought and make someone feel something.

Last year you produced spectacular photos of Shark Bay in Western Australia. These works speak powerfully of the landscape's strong colours and stark land. What drew you to Shark Bay?

Shark Bay is part of a UNESCO World Heritage Site, so its flora and fauna are protected. But amongst this natural landscape is a salt mine (pictured at bottom right), not part of the heritage site, where salt is harvested and exported for human consumption and for use in chemical products.

My project 'Salt and Sky' explores the ways in which humans can physically change the physical appearance of the land. It's a very good example of us taking from the environment. The ponds have gone through a number of expansions, which can lead to the displacement of marine life.

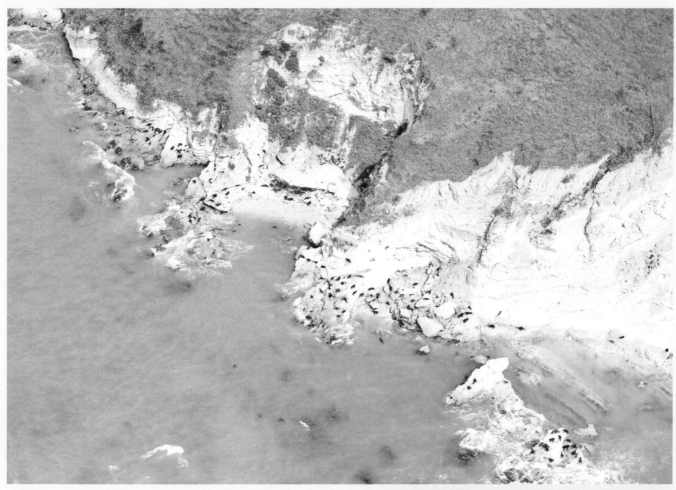

"

Nature finds a way to
make you question
what really matters.

> "We can't fight a volcano with weapons, and we definitely can't buy a new Great Barrier Reef once we eventually destroy it.

> "
> This archipelago
> stands in isolation
> from the rest of the
> world, but it also
> stands for what we
> will lose if we are
> not educated and
> willing to act.

So while viewing aerial images of this aesthetically beautiful human-made place, it's also important to note the sacrifices that were made for it to exist.

Do you constantly challenge yourself to think of new angles and new approaches?

Absolutely. The way I see things and photograph them is very intuitive, so the physical act of shooting comes naturally. I know straight away when I have a shot and when I don't, and there is always an interplay of angles, perspectives, shape, colour, pattern and light. I constantly challenge myself to push the limits, do my research and find places to travel that spark my intrigue and speak to my concerns and desires.

Before the Shark Bay photos, you took a photographic series of the Arctic. What was it like travelling to the cold, far reaches of the world?

My Arctic expedition is something I will never forget. I travelled to Svalbard, an isolated island north of Norway, by myself, where I met a small expedition crew of twelve people. We spent ten days together on the rocking Arctic Ocean, travelling in and out of fjords, breaking through sea ice, witnessing the magnitude of the glaciers and studying polar bears and other wildlife. I stood on the bow of the ship, where at one point I became the northernmost person in the world. Up there, you really get a perspective shift.

The Arctic is constantly in the news as being the place where climate change is most noticeable. Did you find that when you were there? Did you try and capture that with your work?

It is more starkly noticeable, yes. The Arctic warms at least twice as fast as the rest of the world; polar bear numbers are dwindling because the amount of sea ice melting increases each year. They are dependent on the sea ice – they cannot hunt or eat without it, and so many of them end up starving each summer. The glaciers have retreated at alarming rates and the melting permafrost is causing potent methane gases to escape into the atmosphere.

My Arctic series depicts an otherworldly landscape that is in danger of destruction. It's not a place many will see in their lifetime, so I went there to shine light on it by documenting its current state, raising awareness of the imminent threat to its existence.

What do you hope people see when they look at those photos?

I hope they recognise how special the Arctic is. It is such a beautiful, dangerously fragile environment, but it's difficult to enact change if you don't have an appreciation for something. Especially when it's so far away from most people (out of sight, out of mind). This archipelago stands in isolation from the rest of the world, but it also stands for what we will lose if we are not educated and willing to act. My hope is to inspire a growing awareness, at the very least.

You've been to some incredibly diverse places for your artistic practice. How do you choose and plan each location?

It has happened organically so far. I get an idea in my head and I pursue it. Svalbard was always on my list because I remember it appearing in Philip Pullman's novel *Northern Lights*, which I read when I was younger. Other trips have been sparked by pictures I have seen or articles I have read. We are fortunate to have access to imagery of all kinds of places, so I can scope it out before I go.

So ... where to next?

Most likely Greenland, in order to continue my Svalbard and Iceland work. Otherwise, there is a giant list that I just have to tackle one at a time.

..........x

Though photographer Brooke Holm is disturbed by the effects of human action on the natural world, she finds the act of capturing places like Canada a way of shining much needed light on the connection between us and the world we live in – that we are connected, whether it feels that way or not.

The lost art of crossing mountains

Daniel Wakefield Pasley co-founded *Yonder Journal*, an American outdoor magazine that doesn't just talk about adventure in nature, but also studies it, pokes it, prods it, looks at it from all angles and sometimes, just sometimes, attempts to conquer it. Yes, the team behind *Yonder Journal* likes to do things a bit ... differently. That includes setting themselves awe-inspiring and jaw-clenching challenges, like their project Dead Reckoning – an attempt to ride lightweight bicycles across the world's untamed mountain passes in a high-altitude, high-flying series of adventures. Mountains are monumental barriers – but sometimes, in order to evolve and grow and all of those things, you need to dare to cross one or two.

Mountains, historically and culturally speaking, have been one of humankind's biggest and most interesting obstacles when it comes to travel and trade. They're topographically awesome. They're literally and metaphorically breathtaking. And, most importantly, they are fearsome and hazardous, and to tempt their transit can invite dire consequences.

Crossing mountains is in our nature. We are driven to push boundaries, make discoveries and know the unknowable. In other words, we're a risk-taking lot. And as any pioneer – George Donner, Hannibal, Sir Edmund Hillary, Napoleon Bonaparte – could tell you, there is ~~always~~ probably something good on the other side of a mountain: a new language, better cheese, curious musical instruments, gold, rainbows, golden rainbows, etc. But only if you make it over. So please make it over. In the spirit of making it over ...

In 2015 the team behind *Yonder Journal* set out to investigate, document and publish the lost art of Over-Mountain Exploration (O-ME) in an era when people are more interested in climbing mountains than going over them. We called this project Dead Reckoning. For two years we applied the technologies and methodologies of adventure-cycling, bike-packing, and ultra-lightweight touring to multi-day expeditions with a focus on crossing mountains using a variety of trade routes, both ancient and modern. Our investigation of these trade routes took us to New Zealand, Bolivia, Canada, the United States, Australia, Colombia and the Republic of Georgia.

Why a bicycle? Why not a donkey, a motorcycle, a helicopter, a sail boat or simply a pair of hiking boots? Because bicycles are the most pragmatic, useful and efficient means of personal transportation ever invented. They cover ground at the perfect speed, are dependable, simple, adaptable and packable. You have to feed a donkey, put gas in a motorcycle, do so many things to a helicopter. Hiking is so slow. And anyway, have you ever tried sailing a boat over a mountain? Still unconvinced? Think about this: bicycles use the wheel, which is second only to fire in the list of best inventions ever. And we all know fire shouldn't really count.

So was it worth it? Let's see ...

1) Did we discover new cheese flavours and exotic fruits? (Yes, but most of them were gross and flavourless. Colombia has the best fruits in the world. That's not hyperbole: it's science. Just ask for a *jugo con leche*.)

> "
> Crossing mountains is in our nature. We are driven to push boundaries, make discoveries and know the unknowable. In other words, we're a risk-taking lot.

2) Did we really need that yellow fever vaccination? (Probably. We didn't contract yellow fever so, yeah, probably. But we also spent most of our time above 4500 metres [15,000 feet]. Not even yellow fever can survive that kind of elevation.)

3) How much did the helicopter ride in those southern alps cost, anyway? ($1750 USD.)

4) What does it mean to 'work a grizz'? (It's a long story, but can be summed up this way: stare at it, yell at it, back away, but don't back down. Also, shit your pants.)

5) Can it really snow in the middle of North American summer over and over and over and over again? (Yup.)

6) Does altitude sickness mirror or cause – or cause and then mirror – a panic attack? (Double yup. Bonus: extreme altitude also gives you very strange dreams.)

..........x

"

... there is ~~always~~ probably something good on the other side of a mountain: a new language, better cheese, curious musical instruments, gold, rainbows, golden rainbows, etc. But only if you make it over.

Daniel Wakefield Pasley and the team at adventure mag *Yonder Journal* believe that there's always something good to be found on the other side of a mountain. For their project Dead Reckoning, they biked across mountains all over the world just to see what they might find there.

The tradition of stone and steam

....

Growing tired of the capitalist crush and relentless rush of London, artists Holly Gable and Angus Fulton left the city for life on the road, travelling slowly through Europe, then Asia, then back again. They don't live in isolation, but instead experience different cultures, communities and ways of living through work exchange programs. After a few years on the road, Holly and Angus found themselves in Finland, helping prepare a house for winter. They spent a lot of time in the sauna, where they discovered that no connection is stronger than one created in this world of heat and sweat.

There is a Finnish saying: All men are created equal; but nowhere more so than in a sauna.

Naked, climbing up onto a bench. We can vaguely make out the shape of other people in the small, dark room. The smell of hot wood almost scalds our nostrils. We slowly lower ourselves into the heat, skin pressed against the steady, warm wood; it's grounding, holding us. We melt.

Fire crackles. On top of the wood-burning stove is a pile of rocks. Someone dunks a ladle-like scoop into a bucket of water and throws it over them. The water evaporates immediately, sizzling loud. It marks the coming of a wave of hot steam that envelops us from feet to face. We melt some more.

A sauna is a place of softening, calm contemplation and gently spoken words. A sacred space. The act of throwing water to the stones to create the steam cloud is called *löyly* (pronounced LEWle). An ancient word that means 'spirit of life', löyly is a celebration of the elements: fire in the sauna stove, earth in the rocks, water thrown upon them and transformed into air.

After long days restoring Micke and Jouni's old wooden house in southern Finland, time in the sauna was a reward for our bodies and minds. We were preparing the house for winter: climbing it with nail guns, fixing on wooden cladding, painting it with home-cooked linseed oil and building window frames.

Out of the heat, we run down the jetty and into the lake. Time stops in that moment before the panic, before the plunge, with just enough air to breathe. Hot skin meets cold surface in an electric, whole-body rush. As we emerge, eyes and ears at water level, it starts pouring with rain. We can see, hear, taste, feel, smell nothing but the dense rush of plummeting rain droplets hitting the surface of the lake and sending splashes high above our heads. All-encompassing, exhilarating and hilarious. The rain stops and we float around, naked, in the misty silence.

"

We slowly lower ourselves into the heat, skin pressed against the steady, warm wood; it's grounding, holding us. We melt.

> " We were submerged in euphoria; partly because of the sauna-swim-sauna endorphin rush, but mostly because of what we had discovered ...

"

A sauna is a place
of softening, calm
contemplation and
gently spoken words.
A sacred space.

During our time in Finland, we fell in love with Finnish sauna culture. The Finnish think of the sauna like a womb. When settling or moving house, it is the first thing they build.

Dark and meditative, the sauna is a space free of hierarchies in which one should not discuss title or religion. It is a practical place where water is heated for washing, where rye is dried, where meat is cured and malt is prepared. A space for physical and mental cleansing, the soothing of tense muscles and minds. A place to sit together in quiet celebration of our interdependent existence with nature.

When further adventures in Estonia beckoned and the time came for us to say goodbye to our Finnish family, we took a trip to a Helsinki smoke sauna. Cooling off from the heat in the lake, up to our cheeks in the icy September water, we peered at the sun setting through the orange and yellow leaves of autumnal aspen and birch.

We were submerged in euphoria; partly because of the sauna-swim-sauna endorphin rush, but mostly because of what we had discovered: the profound happiness that comes from helping and sharing, and that love, friendship and kindness can be found everywhere.

..........X

Travelling the world on trade

Before starting Pixel Trade, Shantanu Starick was working as a photographer and studying architecture in Australia, travelling overseas one or two times a year. He started Pixel Trade as an experiment to see how long and how far he could travel the world without spending any money, trading his skills as a photographer for bed and board.

The rules of the trade were simple: in exchange for him photographing your project, you would help him travel to your home, give him food and a bed – even help him find the next trade. Four months into the experiment, Shantanu found himself in New York City. It was there he realised that this experiment of his could really work.

He has travelled to every continent, welcomed by strangers into their homes, lives and communities.

What is Pixel Trade?

The Pixel Trade project was an experiment and exploration to see if it was possible to reach all seven continents without spending a cent of my own money on anything in the process.

What inspired you to travel the world without spending any money, and how long did you manage to travel without having any cash?

The inspiration came from a number of circumstances in my life, but it essentially boiled down to a desire to challenge everyday ideas, such as the barriers we put in place that create a perception that something is unachievable. Money was a big one. I love it – most people do – but I don't agree that it is as important as many of us think. The core of what money offers is amazing, but the dependencies and stress it can often build up are not. Perception was the main thing in question here.

After 1238 days, I managed to reach all seven continents without spending a cent.

What did you have in your backpack?

I think travelling with no money or very little money is associated with backpacking and hostels or couch surfing, but Pixel Trade wasn't that. I travelled well, I stayed in comfort and I ate like a king the majority of the time. I felt so privileged to see the world for such a long time without having to feel I was on a budget and watching my savings. The result was that I travelled with a big roller suitcase, camera bag and laptop bag. I didn't travel light. I didn't need to, most of the time. I had to be ready for every climate, so my bags were focused on equipment and versatility.

At what point during Pixel Trade did you realise, 'Hang on, this is going really well, I'm just going to keep doing this'?

It was always on and off. The first time I felt it was in New York City, around month four of the project. That place makes you feel like a rock star when it flows with you and a total washout when it doesn't. NYC was in my flow, and it gave me a boost of how unreal the life I was living truly was.

When you first started the project, how did you get offers for trades? And did the number of trades increase as your project went on?

All I needed to do was start with one trade. Part of the 'rules' was that the person I was trading with had to find me the next trade if I didn't have one, until which time I would be in their care. Word spread over time, and things started to get more demanding, which meant more emails and more organising. It was great because yes, I could be picky, but it also became more draining. By the final year of the project I was booked out four to six months ahead.

How did moving around so much change your relationship to place and nature?

Drastically. Political borders started to blur into one another. New places I had never seen started to feel familiar in a bizarre way, which for me wasn't a good thing because I would stop looking when it came to photographing my surroundings. I had to concentrate and remind myself how unique these places were.

"

It essentially boiled down to a desire to challenge everyday ideas, such as the barriers we put in place that create a perception that something is unachievable.

Nature became such an important refuge for me too. If I was disconnected for too long, my energy began to falter. By default it was easier for people in cities to trade with me, and therefore most of my trades happened around large metropolitan areas. A city is wild in a way that can suck your energy away. I didn't have a lot left to give, so I started holding nature as a liferaft.

Did living in foreign countries without money change the way you connected with each place?

I never looked into tourist attractions, shopping areas, bars, restaurants … anything that involved money, I wasn't interested in knowing about. I was brought to those environments with my trades, but I was more interested in exploring what the physical area offered, not the products and services therein. I was also lucky as my trades wanted to be great hosts and they knew the area they lived in better than someone who just passes through. They wanted to show me a good time, so I really got to experience things from a local perspective. Which to me is travel. My experience of a local's experience.

Did the people you trade with have a similar ethos on living and money?

Sometimes, but it was more about people who welcomed different forms of thinking. I traded with wealthy people and poor people. They are the same, in most ways. We forget that sometimes.

What is your current project?

The Honorarium Volumes. It is an idea that came from my last trade to Antarctica. The volumes are an ongoing collection of limited edition photographic artworks that focus on small interactions all over the world. Each volume is focused on a particular country and is funded by an audience who pre-purchases a print package or book.

..........x

> **"**
> A city is wild in a way that can suck your energy away. I didn't have a lot left to give, so I started holding nature as a liferaft.

Shantanu Starick travelled all over the world, experiencing landscapes like this one in Austria, but didn't spend a cent: instead he took photographs of people's homes and projects in exchange for room and board. In this way he saw all seven continents, discovering that money isn't the barrier we like to think it is.

Wild creations

Chef and adventurer Sarah Glover grew up in one of Australia's wildest places, surfing the turbulent waves of Tasmania, nibbling on berries from the bushes she passed. Fresh, local produce was always on her table and blooming in her backyard. With wilderness so close, she didn't have to go far for adventure.

The thrill of far-flung adventures was what drew her to the mainland, where she met people who inspired her love of surfing, travel and cooking for people. As she made her way up the coast of Australia, then on to New York City and back again, she helped open restaurants and design menus, learning about cooking along the way. She opened her own sweets shop in Bondi Beach, Australia, in 2009, spending her days in the surf and pouring herself into cooking and sharing.

The more people she met, the more she found that most of them hadn't grown up as wild as she had – had never known the joys that come from cooking outdoors with family and friends. So she wrote her *Wild Adventure Cookbook*, dedicated to the art and pleasures of cooking outdoors and over the campfire with good friends, local ingredients and the good that comes of letting nature inspire you.

You grew up in Tasmania – what was your childhood there like, and how did it influence your love of food and the outdoors?

Growing up on the island, I never thought twice about having fresh raspberries at my beck and call, or apricots that oozed with every golden, sun-filled bite. My backyard was full of fresh produce, which I could eat whenever my tummy grumbled, and the wild outdoors were at my doorstep. It wasn't so much of an influence as a way of living. You went outside on the weekends; you surfed rugged beaches and lit fires to keep warm.

It wasn't until I moved to the mainland that I started to realise that my experience having access to local, fresh produce was a rarity for most.

How does surfing inspire you?

Surfing is my time to clear my mind. It allows me to stop thinking about what I need to do or be and to just laugh and have fun. Fun and laughter are medicine – they motivate me. The friends I have met through the ocean have become lifelong mates who inspire me to be authentic.

What drew you to pack your bags and go up the coast of Australia, then over to America? What continues to drive you to go on adventures?

I am a thrill seeker – I can't help myself. I'm always trying to find a new challenge and hurdle to jump over, because it's an adrenaline rush. I just like creating and being on the road – it stimulates my creativity. I go home to sleep and rest, then I go out again.

You've worn many professional hats over the years, both food related and not. What keeps drawing you back to food?

I like to talk, to hear people's stories and share my passion with them. For me, cooking is about that exchange. Food is what I can offer people. I think it's that I get to be creative with my hands.

Food is something that nourishes and brings people together. It is a necessity of life, and I want to deliver it in a way that inspires people to gather. The campfire is a nonjudgmental environment – people take off their shoes and just relax. You don't find people looking at their phones around a fire!

"

My backyard was
full of fresh produce,
which I could eat
whenever my tummy
grumbled, and the wild
outdoors were at my
doorstep. It wasn't so
much of an influence
as a way of living.

You talk about 'raw cooking' – being inspired not by a recipe, but by the ingredients you have to work with. What do you love about that approach to cooking?

I like the challenge of cooking with what I find on the road or at the markets, talking to the providers about their produce and what makes them happy. It's about the story and the connections you make. I come from a long line of farmers and fishermen, and the tales and stories they tell make the food taste better. Sounds weird, but it's true.

You have a cookbook that's all about wild cooking – the idea of cooking outside and out on adventures. What inspired that project? What do you hope your readers will take away from it?

I grew up living in the bush, playing up trees and eating food from the garden, so I think it was meant to be that my first book would pay homage to that way of life. It was so much fun just taking it outdoors, not knowing what I was going to cook, but just creating from the moment. I think that life has become too sterile. We have forgotten what it's like to get your hands dirty and let go of the rules.

What does nature mean to you and your work?

Without it, we wouldn't be able to breathe; we need the land to survive and we need to respect it! I wouldn't be doing what I am without it, so it's everything.

..........x

"

I think that life has become too sterile. We have forgotten what it's like to get your hands dirty and let go of the rules.

Mussels with salt water and potatoes

It's magical, making this dish by the sea with freshly caught mussels plucked straight from the rocks. We were on a beach on the east coast of Tasmania when we tried this method, at a little bay we'd discovered by accident. It was sheltered from the sea breeze, the perfect spot to light a campfire. I stoked the fire to a medium heat while preparing my mussels – once ready, I buried the pot in the coals. The air filled with a smoky aroma that drew my friends in from the beach to sit around and share a meal with the sea on our side.

Remember to pick mussels whose shells are securely closed and that are damp and shiny. If you have to purchase the mussels, don't pick any with broken, cracked or split shells. This dish is so easy; I promise you anyone can make it.

Serves 3

1 onion, finely diced

2 tomatoes, diced

3 salad rose potatoes (or another variety of red-skinned potato), skin on, cut into 1 cm (⅓ in) cubes

2 cups white wine

1 cup seawater

1 kg (2 lb 3 oz) mussels, cleaned and debearded

2 cloves fresh young garlic, diced (for garnish)

small handful of flat-leaf parsley, leaves picked and washed (for garnish)

Light a campfire and let it burn down until it's at medium heat.

Combine the onion and tomatoes in your billy or large pot and place them in the coals of the fire. Cook for about 1 minute, then add the potatoes, white wine and 1 cup seawater.

Cook for 20 minutes or until the potatoes are soft.

Add the mussels, then cover and cook until the mussels open up, discarding any that don't open (they are not good to eat).

Serve sprinkled with garlic and parsley. Eat at the beach and enjoy the salty air and salty mussels.

Campfire marshmallows

There's something comforting, something heartening, about putting a marshmallow on a stick and roasting it over a crackling fire until it's just bubbling on the outside, its skin turned toasty and fire-edged. You can make your own marshmallows before you leave home, which will give you the satisfaction of making it, as well as roasting it, yourself.

1 cup water

3 packets gelatine

2 cups white sugar

½ cup corn syrup

1 tbsp vanilla extract

1 tbsp peppermint extract

chocolate for a dark, gooey centre (optional)

icing sugar, for dusting

Get a slice tin ready by greasing it with butter and lining it with cling wrap.

Pour ½ cup of the water into a medium bowl. Add the gelatine, stir and set aside.

In a medium saucepan on high heat, place the sugar, corn syrup and the remaining ½ cup of water. Bring to the boil (you want it to roll with bubbles). Allow to boil for an additional minute, then remove from the heat. Add in the vanilla and peppermint extracts.

Using a handheld electric mixer, begin mixing the gelatine mixture. Slowly add the sugar syrup while you continue to mix on a low speed.

Once all sugar syrup is added, turn the mixer to high speed and whip for 10-12 minutes until the batter almost triples in size and becomes very thick. Scrape down the sides to prevent overflowing.

Transfer the mixture into your prepared slice tin – work fast, or it will set before it's all in the pan. If you like, you can pour only half of the mixture into the pan, then spread melted chocolate over it, leaving the edges white, and cover with the remaining mixture to create what will be gooey chocolate insides. Once you've finished pouring everything in, cover with more cling wrap and set the pan aside to set.

Once it is set, place icing sugar on a board, turn out the marshmallow and cut into chunks.

Lentil and Matt Purbrick moved from the city to the country, transforming an old, run-down property into the farmhouse of their dreams. It's there they learnt how to live with nature, devoting their days to growing their own food, tending their animals, and boiling life down to its simplest pleasures.

The joys of growing, trading, sustaining

It was the prospect of living a real life – a full life – that enticed Lentil and Matt Purbrick to quit their jobs in the city and move to the Australian country. They were after something different, a chance to connect with food, people, time and nature. They fixed up a derelict old house that overlooked a billabong and planted a world that grew and grew and grew. They shared this world through their food, their trades, and their blogging – inspiring thousands of others to think about how they, too, could live a more sustainable life.

You live in a house on a pocket of a bigger property. What's the house like, and what sort of state was it in when you found it?

Matt and I live in a very old farmhouse; it was originally built in 1940. It's a cute little weatherboard cottage that overlooks the property's backwater, which is like a billabong (a small, quiet water hole). The house is full of white walls, wood, a little bit of art from people we love, a whole lot of pottery, books and linen. It's just got the simple things that we love. It's surrounded by a hectare (2.5 acres) of cleared land, where we grow all of our produce and keep our animals, and just over a hectare of native bush.

I still remember what the house and property was like before we moved in. We actually had to climb in through the window because there wasn't a key for the door. It was so run-down that the power points were coming out of the walls, many of which were cracked, and it was filled with old linoleum floors and a bathroom that looked like it had walked straight out of a '60s motel (and not in a good way). The outside had so many sheds that people had half-built over the years and heaps of junk. But it had a great feeling about it, so we cleaned it up and made it ours.

Did you fix it up yourself?

We renovated it ourselves, quickly, over one winter. We wanted to get the farm planted before the summer, so we made it happen. We basically just ripped out a whole heap of stuff to bring it back to a simple shell, took out a few walls to open it up, painted it white and filled it with wooden benches and a deck. We took out all of the sheds that blocked our view of the billabong and repurposed (or got rid of) the materials that were lying around. Then we built our garden and moved our animals in! We made it an open, functional space, and we really opened it up to the outside so it was much more connected to the land it was on.

Did you move to the house with the aim of becoming self-sustaining, or did you sort of make it up as you went along?

I wouldn't say we are truly self-sustaining: it's not really something we see as achievable or realistic. We definitely believe in doing what you can, and sharing/trading your abundance with the 'village' so everyone has what they need.

> **"**
> The main aim, always, is that we work with nature – what it is doing at any given time.

“
We see our lives ruled by
nature, our lives change
with nature – rather than
the other way around.

But yes, we definitely made it up as we went along, to a point. I think you have to – you only know what you know at any given time. As you learn, you become more open to different ideas, your perspective changes and your passion for different things develops. We learnt and experimented with all of the things we could do ourselves. The main thing for us was, and still is, the *experience* of it – growing, gathering, nurturing animals, trading, making what we could. That's what it is all about. This, for us, is just so rewarding and life-changing.

How do you run your property?

The main aim, always, is that we work with nature – what it is doing at any given time. We see it as a dance: it does this, you do that. You are always watching it and responding to it. We think that agriculture, as a rule, has become too controlling. It is not so much about cooperating with nature anymore as it is about dominating and enslaving it. So we try to keep things a bit wilder. We try to give our animals what they need and then let them live according to their instincts, not our constant interference. It's the same with our plants. We try to just give them the optimal conditions to thrive naturally, and then we let them grow and do their thing, again interfering as little as possible.

It means less work for us and provides us with incredible results. We're not doing anything more or less special than constantly observing our plants and animals and ensuring they have everything they need. There aren't any rules, just simple observation and response.

Has working the land changed your connection with nature?

It has one hundred per cent changed it. We see our lives ruled by nature, our lives change with nature – rather than the other way around.

This is how we have come to understand the world. Whether we are at home or travelling, we are always observing – looking for what's flowering around us, what fruit is ripening, what insects are doing. We understand the time of year, the season, the climate. It's how we make sense of things all the time and live *with* nature.

What is an average day on the farm?

Unlike what many may think, we take the mornings slow. We have a juice, a coffee or a tea and make a slow breakfast. Then we get out there and do what needs to be done – it can be anything from planting seeds, harvesting, gathering from the wild, tending to the animals. It is always changing,

> " Everything feels abundant – it just feels as though we have so *much*. So much to be grateful for, so much beauty, so much food around us. It's hard to get that until you surround yourself with nature.

depending on the time of year. We just know, based on what time of year it is, what needs to be done.

We try to limit our time on computers and only check our emails twice a week. But we also love projects – we are, at heart, artists. So we write, draw, paint, do pottery, dance, photograph. Some of this we get paid for or trade for, and some we just do for fun. This also inspires our outside time – it all fits together.

Besides growing your own food, you also cook it and sometimes even trade it – how important is it to you to create and share things made with your own hands?

Very. This is where the joy is at; to us, it is what makes life fun. If we can't grow or produce something ourselves, then having a direct relationship with the people who do is important to us because we've seen how enriching that experience is.

If someone took away our ability to cook, trade, feast, I truly think we would become very depressed. Those shared experiences are what life's all about!

How do you feel stepping out of the door in the morning and seeing the land that you work on?

Peaceful, and as if we can breathe. Everything feels abundant – it just feels as though we have so *much*. So much to be grateful for, so much beauty, so much food around us. It's hard to get that until you surround yourself with nature. Nature is naturally abundant, whereas the urban environment can feel inherently competitive.

Your journey has become famous through your blog, social media, events and now your book, and you've become advocates for a more sustainable way of living. How does that advocacy shape what you do?

It's probably the other way around; all of our decisions have shaped our advocacy. Whom we work with, what we choose to do in our everyday lives, how we travel and the stories we share have always had sustainable values at their core. It's something we've always embraced in all aspects of our lives. It's like art to us. It's our passion and something we live for.

We truly believe in what we do and we genuinely live by what we advocate. But we are not driven by our advocacy.

We are driven simply by the aim to live a good life. It just so happens that in living a good life we seem to be inspiring others to make positive changes in theirs. We feel super lucky by how all that has turned out.

At the end of the day, what makes you satisfied?

Feeling satisfied in all of life's small moments. Feeling grateful for everything we have and all of the experiences that make up life – a morning coffee, harvesting some tomatoes, smelling fresh air, love, people, plants, cooking …

This is our measure: if we are doing things that make us feel negative or we aren't enjoying, we stop. It's about the everyday things for us.

..........x

Foraging for happiness

What would you do for work if money, career or years of study weren't part of the equation? Elle Nikishkova started out following an interest in international relations, but when her life took an unexpected turn, she found her priorities had changed. She started appreciating other things in life – exploring the Swedish wilderness, foraging for mushrooms and learning bushcraft in the forest – and suddenly, she had to re-evaluate what she once thought was important; what really made her happy. This simple question led to a career change that melded happiness in a life outdoors with her calling: open fire cooking.

I always knew that I wanted to work in politics. As a teenager, I was involved in various environmental groups, NGOs and a local political party. At seventeen, I was picked to join the Swedish delegation to the UN Climate Change conference as a youth representative. Basically my entire existence was dedicated to making political changes for a better world.

At university, I chose to study political science and economic history. After years of intensive academia and the occasional backpacking break, I finished my Master of International Studies and started working in international relations and human rights. But, as we all know, life can take unexpected turns, rearranging thoughts and plans that seemed so natural before.

Approximately halfway through my studies, my mum got diagnosed with cancer, and after a long time of illness and various treatments, she passed away. It was a painful experience, and the consequent end to an era, but it also gave birth to a new beginning: it opened my mind to new prospects and perspectives. When you follow someone to the end of the road and have to say goodbye standing on the edge of a cliff, you realise how fragile life is – you need to enjoy it while you can.

Thoughts about life and happiness made me question my chosen career path. Would I do this if I knew that there was no tomorrow? And if there was no tomorrow, what would I do today?

The answer was simple: I would hang out in the woods with some friends by the campfire, cook tasty meals and forage for mushrooms and other exciting edible plants. I would drink beer, enjoy the company and bask in the beauty of nature. Eventually I decided to do just this, not because there is no tomorrow, but because this was what really made me happy. I turned my happy place into my work.

Nowadays, I am an outdoor chef who specialises in open fire cooking. I can set up my mobile outdoor kitchen wherever I want: in the forests of northern Sweden, up in the mountains bordering Norway, or alongside glittering lakes or flowering fragrant meadows in the south of Sweden.

"

The key to bushcraft is to gain the skill and understanding that enables you to transform from an observer to an experienced participant.

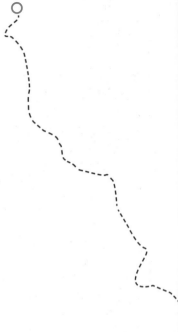

The art of open fire cooking mastered by our ancestors has fallen into oblivion in our increasingly technological world. Yet this development that has alienated us from nature has also given us an urge to find our way back to our roots: to enjoy the simple things, offline and off-grid. Back when neither shopping centres nor pharmacies existed, we would source food and medicine in the wild. Even though our forests don't look the same today, loads of amazing fruits of nature can be foraged just around the corner, as almost 70 per cent of Sweden is covered by forests. During summertime and through to late autumn, the forests are full of edible plants: blueberries, lingonberries, cloudberries, cranberries and wild cherries; nettles, wood sorrel, dandelions and an abundance of edible mushrooms. The woods are full of nutritious, organic foods that can be foraged and used in healthy meals and drinks.

Other old knowledge is being revived with new epithets, such as bushcraft – a growing trend among outdoor enthusiasts. Learning how to build a shelter, make up a fire and forage for edible plants might take some time, but once you have this knowledge, nature can be your comfortable new home. The key to bushcraft is to gain the skill and understanding that enables you to transform from an observer to an experienced participant. The more you know about nature, the more confident and comfortable you become in exploring it further.

In Sweden, Allemansrätt – the Right of Public Access, or the 'freedom to roam' – is a principle protected by law that gives everyone the right to explore in nature; you can camp, forage, hike or kayak freely across the country, with just commonsense rules to protect both land and landowner. Endless miles of adventure lie at our feet, as long as we show respect for the plants and animals living here.

As the interest to explore the outdoors grows, my task is to teach and inspire, bringing more people to an even more positive experience. Through foraging courses, open fire cooking workshops, outdoor events and social media, I get to meet and educate a lot of eager nature lovers, and together we create great memories in the outdoors. This is what life is all about: having fun while learning new things, exploring and making yourself and others happy.

..........X

A simple open fire meal for winter or summer

Even though foraging is a big part of my job, I don't use only forest ingredients when I cook. To promote and support sustainable food production, I try to source my ingredients from local farmers and food suppliers that engage in responsible agriculture. All over Sweden there are small producers of tasty treats, beautiful vegetables, flavourful cheeses, traditionally smoked meats and exciting drinks. These products are often sold from small barns in the middle of nowhere – finding these is an adventure in itself.

Another aspect of food sustainability is to try to live and eat with the seasons. During the foraging season for plants and mushrooms I pick loads and preserve for later: drying nettles and herbs, pickling mushrooms and making jams and cordials. This way the foraged goods can be enjoyed year-round.

The following recipe is simple and delicious. It consists of locally grown potatoes, onions, garlic, herbs, wild forest mushrooms and juniper berries. It's a beautiful umami-rich meal that can be made in winter or summer over an open fire.

Serves 4

Oil or butter for frying
1 handful dried mushrooms
1 kg (2 lb 3 oz) potatoes, cut into wedges
2 onions, diced
5–10 juniper berries, crushed
3 garlic cloves, crushed
Parsley, to garnish

Soak the dried mushrooms in 1 cup of water. In this recipe I use a mix of porcini (*Boletus edulis*) and black trumpets (*Craterellus cornucopioides*). If you do not have forest mushrooms, buying from a store will work just fine.

In a wide pan, fry the potato wedges in oil or butter until they are crisp. Add the onions on the side and fry until golden.

Move the potatoes and onions to one side, then add the mushrooms with the water they have been soaked in. Let the mushrooms simmer until the water has evaporated, then mix in with the rest.

Add the juniper berries and garlic. Fry for a couple of minutes before adding the parsley and seasoning with salt and pepper.

Enjoy this meal with good company in a beautiful place.

"
We wanted to stay there for a long time, to get the feeling of living there, not just visiting.

The heart of darkness

Inge Wegge was born into the cold, wild places of the world and feels called to document their precarious beauty.

His first film, *North of the Sun*, was made with his friend Jørn Ranum in 2012 and followed their stay on a remote, uninhabited cove off the north coast of Norway, far north of the Arctic Circle where the sun disappears for months at a time. Even though this beach was in the far reaches of the world, it was covered in pieces of plastic that had washed ashore. They built a hut from this material and settled down to live through the dark winter, surfing and attempting to clean up the beach.

But Inge was not finished with these wild yet tarnished places. In his second film, *Bear Island*, Inge travelled to the uninhabited Bear Island to surf with his brothers Hakon and Markus. While the brothers were told to leave no trace, they arrived to beaches already covered in trash. In Inge's film, we voyeur on the fate of these places where humans leave a trace without making a footprint.

Tell us about yourself and where you live.

I live on the island of Lofoten in Norway. It's a paradise for me. It has everything I can dream of: mountains for skiing, snowboarding and climbing, good waves for surfing, and the people here are really nice. We live on an island, and island people tend to take care of each other.

My fantastic and inspiring wife is also into surfing and climbing, so we often do things together out in nature. Our daughter is three years old, and we have a second child coming soon. I'm really looking forward to taking them on adventures.

How did you come up with the idea for your first film, *North of the Sun*?

My friend from film school and I had both been to this amazing beach and seen all the trash and materials laying around. It inspired us to live there, building a house from the things that had washed ashore. We wanted to stay there for a long time, to get the feeling of *living* there, not just visiting. We knew the waves were surfable and we wanted to stay over one winter season so we could really enjoy it.

Both of your films feature places that few humans have ever set foot on, and yet they're covered in human-made waste. How do you feel when you arrive at a remote, wild place to find it covered in trash?

It's sad. It makes me realise how much plastic there must be in our oceans. Only a small part of it ends up on the beaches; the rest is just floating around, being crushed into smaller and smaller pieces, ending up inside fish and animals that might become our food someday.

***North of the Sun* is an adventure story, but there is also a strong environmental message. Was that unintentional, or was that part of the plan?**

It came naturally. The place is so beautiful, but I felt sad seeing all the plastic washed up on the beach. We wanted to clean everything. Absolutely everything. So we started picking up the pieces. But when we dug down into the sand, we discovered that it was just layers and layers of plastic. And new trash just kept coming in, every day. We realised that we could never take it all away. We wanted to make people aware of it and inspire them to try and make a difference.

In what way does 'giving back to nature' enhance an adventure, particularly in such a remote part of the world?

Nature gives me so many good moments. We wanted to give something back to it – not just consume what it offered. There was something about the feeling of a clean beach at the end of all that work. It made me feel that I had earned the right to call the bay my home.

Most surfers seek out tropical islands for their surf trips, but for *Bear Island* you chose what must be one of the world's coldest. Why did you choose it?

Warm places are tempting, but we don't know that much about snakes and mosquitoes and stuff. We are used to the cold, so it was natural for us to look north. Maybe it's a Norwegian thing, exploring cold places. Bear Island looked like the perfect place. It's a small island, only 15 kilometres (9 miles) wide and 20 kilometres (12 miles) long, so we had the chance to explore the whole coastline. Its mountains looked perfect for playing in the snow.

There's a moment in *Bear Island* when you talk about waves only existing for one moment in time, so to surf them is to coexist with that one pulse of the ocean's power. What does nature's power teach you?

When I'm out for a long time, I realise things that might feel important in everyday life – answering emails, staying updated on social media – really aren't. I also see more details in nature and become more open to its impressions. Living a rich life with simple means. Surfing is special because there is so much power in a wave, and becoming one with that energy makes me so focused. It makes every second feel like ten.

..........X

"

There was something about the feeling of a clean beach at the end of all that work. It made me feel that I had earned the right to call the bay my home.

Inge Wegge and Jørn Ranum chose to live on a sunless, frigid beach in northern Norway because they wanted to truly get to know it. They built their house out of the trash that had washed up on shore, then spent their days surfing and cleaning up a place that, for a while, came to feel like home.

Nature's many compositions

Bec Kilpatrick grew up photographing the ocean and sugarcane fields of Byron Bay in New South Wales, Australia, on her dad's old Canon film camera. It was the start of her love of photography, which she developed at school, holing away in the darkroom at lunch and watching as the chemical process unveiled the scenes she had captured. She found that photography wasn't just about the magic of capturing a moment, but also about process, planning and practice. Once she started travelling, she discovered that taking her art on the road and out into nature helped her connect with her surroundings and inspire others to do the same.

Can you tell us about your work as a nature photographer?

All of my work begins with wanting to explore something in greater detail: a landscape through the lens of my camera, or the small textures of a bird's feather when I draw. A lot of my photography is based around nature, but also how we interact with it. I also shoot a lot of weddings, and try to draw and paint as much as I can. It's quite busy and transient, but I wouldn't want it any other way. My photographs often capture some sort of adventure, whether it's driving across the country, hiking in the mountains or exploring a new landscape in a new country. My biggest drive to photograph comes from seeing and experiencing a new place.

You're an illustrator as well. How do these two artistic practices differ and align?

Whether I'm taking photos or drawing, both processes involve me quietly observing and trying to represent a subject in a new way for people to enjoy. While both influence each other and demand the same patience, they do have their differences. With a photograph, you are bound by what you put in the frame; it is a constant challenge to create new perspectives and interesting compositions. When drawing, you are limitless. Whatever comes into your mind is possible, and that freedom can be liberating or terrifying. For me, it's important to have balance, to keep inspired and play with the way both mediums interact with each other.

Where do you live, and what do you enjoy about splitting your time between two continents?

I grew up in Byron Bay and will always call the sound of waves home. I travelled to Canada when I was twenty-one, where I fell in love with mountains (and Andrew, my partner). Since then we have moved between Calgary and Byron Bay, shooting weddings in the summers and working on travel and lifestyle jobs. More recently, we've been setting up market booths across Canada, selling our artwork and photographs. It has been such a fun and refreshing way to interact with people and share our art. These days it's so easy to get caught up with posting online and feeling disconnected with the work you are putting out. By getting out in the community and talking with other artists, we feel a greater connection with the work we are creating – it gives it meaning. We are so lucky to be able to split our time between two countries and work year-round doing what we love (with lots of time for exploring, too).

> " I never regret travelling to a new place. You always learn so much from the environment you step into and the people you meet.

What's a normal day like for you?

Every day begins with a cup of tea! Sometimes it's in bed with my favourite cup, and other times it's in a travel mug on a long road trip. My favourites are made on a camp stove on top of a mountain after watching a beautiful sunrise.

I really struggle to impose structure on my day-to-day life, as freelancing can leave you always working. I'm always trying to figure out the best balance between creating new work, travelling for content, keeping up-to-date with websites and social content, and meeting my deadlines.

Your shots of nature are incredible and inspire us to dream of new places – how much work goes into each shot?

I never regret travelling to a new place. You always learn so much from the environment you step into and the people you meet. If I can convince someone looking at my photos to get outside and explore something outside their comfort zone, then that's amazing.

There's always a lot of planning that goes into photography, particularly in the realm of seeking out good locations. I am always researching to figure out when the light will be best, when the sun rises or sets, where the moon is and just generally keeping up-to-date on what the weather is doing. You have to set yourself up so that the unpredictable and unknown can create the magic shots.

How important is nature to your work?

As important as it is to my wellbeing. I never identified with life in the city; I either wanted to be an artist or a biologist when I grew up. The patterns, systems and cycles that exist in nature are fascinating, and I have fallen in love with documenting and interpreting them in my work. It's so nice to be reminded to stop and notice the little things that often go unnoticed in our world every day.

Where do you go in nature when you need to recharge?

When I'm at home in Australia, straight to my local beach. There's nothing more comforting than going for a swim in the ocean and losing my thoughts on the horizon. On the other hand, my ideal escape is to go on a long camping adventure in the mountains. I'm so grateful to have been able to spend so much time exploring the Rocky Mountains in Canada. There is nothing more grounding than packing a bag full of food and camping gear and sleeping under the stars for a few nights. It's the perfect way to reset your mind about the things that really matter, and it's where I feel most inspired.

> **"**
> There is nothing more grounding than packing a bag full of food and camping gear and sleeping under the stars for a few nights. It's the perfect way to reset your mind about the things that really matter, and it's where I feel most inspired.

What are some of your top tips for taking great photographs in nature?

First, the time of day is crucial. The best light comes in the early morning and late afternoon when the sun is low and soft. In order to take advantage of this light, you need to plan your days around it. Be prepared to be out late and get up early, and always pack a headlamp for those moments when you're setting up or heading back to camp after getting your shot!

Remember that the perfect shot requires planning, but make sure to plan for the unexpected. I put so much planning into capturing a 'perfect' shot, but some of my favourite images have come out of crazy adventures on little to no sleep! Like when planning out how to get a shot of the Emerald Lakes along the Tongariro Crossing on New Zealand's North Island (pictured at right). I read it was a three-hour hike from the carpark to the Red Crater, the highest point of the Crossing, and its spectacular view of the three turquoise-coloured volcanic lakes. We wanted to catch the first light hitting the lakes with no one around, so we began our hike around three in the morning to make sure we had plenty of time to hike up and find the perfect spot to set up our tripods. It was pitch black with no moon to guide us, my headlamp was running out of battery power and the wind was intense. We pushed through regardless and ended up getting to the top of the Red Crater around five: an hour-and-a-half before the sun was set to rise. We huddled together, trying to stay warm, when all of a sudden some hot air hit us. We thought we were losing our minds until we remembered that we were on volcanic land, which was steaming. When the sun finally rose over the volcanoes, we got the most beautiful photographs of the first light on the lakes and the steam rising in the foreground. It was a magical morning.

Make sure to get to know your camera and how to use it in different conditions. There's something to be said for the phrase, 'The best camera is the one you have with you'. Most people carry around pretty good cameras in their pockets every day – their phones! Smartphones do take great photos, but if you want to go beyond that and learn how to control and manipulate an image, a DSLR is a must.

DSLR means 'Digital Single Lens Reflex' or, to put it more simply, a camera that uses mirrors and interchangeable lenses. They aren't cheap or light, but the quality and control of the images gives it an advantage over any other compact camera. Using a DSLR allows you to control the shutter speed, aperture and overall exposure of your image. Controlling the shutter speed allows you to manipulate how long the digital sensor is exposed to light, allowing you to freeze or drag movement. Controlling the aperture allows you to adjust the diameter of the opening that lets light in. The lower the aperture, the wider the opening. For example, F1.8 lets more light in than F22, and it allows you to use the camera in low light situations. Once you learn how to use shutter speed and aperture, you can make sure your image is exposed properly for your environment.

There is no 'best' setting for your camera: just the most appropriate for a given situation. You always have to be ready to manually adjust your settings to the ever-changing environment. If the wind suddenly picks up on top of a mountain, it helps to switch your camera to Shutter Priority at a speed of at least 1/500 of a second. Shutter Priority, labelled 'TV' on your camera, allows you to choose a shutter speed and will automatically pick the correct aperture. This setting makes sure you have a shutter speed fast enough to overcome the camera shake caused by heavy winds. There's nothing worse than getting back to your computer and realising your photos aren't sharp!

Think about composition. It's easy to just point and shoot when you're in a beautiful place, but it's worth pausing to think about framing your shot. Take a second to note your surrounds: what objects or shapes make up the foreground? Would the photo be more interesting with someone in the frame to show scale? What lines are naturally present to lead your eye through the image?

In a traditional landscape photo, you have three fields of view: the foreground, the middle ground and the background. You can guide the viewer's eye to each of these areas using different techniques. The most popular is the rule of thirds, which I will talk about below. You can also use a low aperture to make sure only one field of view is in focus, isolating the focal point of the image: for instance, keeping

the middle ground with a lighthouse in focus but blurring the foreground (rocks) and background (sky). Another way you can direct the focus is by using the natural lines in the landscape to 'lead the eye through the image'.

There are a lot of compositional rules in photography that I think should be explored, then broken. The most popular is the rule of thirds, where you visually split up your image into a grid of nine squares and place your focal point at one of the horizontal and vertical intersections. The focal point is what you want the viewer to focus on first – it creates a powerful image. For landscape photography, it's nice to play with this rule by putting the horizon either in the top third or bottom third of your image. Try and avoid putting your horizon in the centre – use the grid to experiment with where you place it. For instance, if you want to capture a surfing photo, you could have the sea horizon running along the top third, the sun setting in the top left intersection and the surfer paddling on the bottom right intersection (this would be the main focal point).

When framing a shot, the main thing I think about is simplicity. It's often challenging to try and strip a busy landscape scene back to something uncluttered and captivating, but I think the most powerful images are often the simplest ones.

> **"**
> I put so much planning into capturing a 'perfect' shot, but some of my favourite images have come out of crazy adventures on little to no sleep!

Try out different lenses. There are two different types of lenses for DSLR cameras: fixed and zoom. Fixed, also called a prime lens, has just one focal length, which you cannot adjust. It tends to focus more quickly and produce sharper images, although you have less freedom when it comes to composition. A zoom lens is made with a focal range so you can shift in and out, which allows you more control when it comes to framing your image – much better for landscape photography.

There are lenses made for specific uses, like wide-angle for shooting landscapes and telephoto for shooting wildlife, but it's important to experiment. Don't always reach for your wide-angle lens; some of my favourite photos have come from trying out a telephoto lens.

Use a tripod. A tripod is essential for minimising camera shake and ensuring your images are nice and crisp, especially when taking photos in low light when the shutter needs to be open for longer in order to let in enough light to get a good image. You can also use your camera's settings to create some lovely stylistic effects when using your tripod. For example, if you are shooting water, stabilising your camera on a tripod lets you leave your shutter open for longer, allowing all the water's ripples and textures to blur and look like glass.

Play around. Don't be afraid to try new things and experiment. Try different shutter speeds to capture movement and different apertures to add a focal point. This is the only way you are going to get to know your camera and create a style that's unique to you.

..........X

Bec Kilpatrick splits her time between the mountains of Canada and the beaches of Australia, chasing photographs of nature in all its many forms. During a trip to Tongariro National Park on New Zealand's North Island, she was reminded that it's worth getting up for sunrises and sticking around for chilly sunsets for the chance to capture images like these.

What's washed ashore

James Herman grew up in Oregon in the United States, but it wasn't until he reached his twenties that he stumbled across the coast's driftwood forts. These ad-hoc, temporary structures are forts of all kinds, from teepees to shacks, made from the driftwood that washes up on the beach. They are a local tradition built for shelter from the wind, to protect campfires, or simply for the pleasure of building.

Driftwood forts represent the hardy self-build culture of the Pacific Northwest, a theme explored in manifestos like Lloyd Kahn's *Shelter* and the *Whole Earth Catalog*. James devoured these books growing up, and his art has increasingly revolved around self-building. He documented these forts through photos and by recording lists of the materials they contained, eventually posting them online. For James, this isn't just about art; it's also a paean to self-build culture, which he continued to explore when he and his friends built a studio on a property in Los Angeles, surrounded by fruit trees and land he happily tends.

How did your interest in driftwood forts begin?

I was walking down the beach in Lincoln City, Oregon, where I was doing an artist residency. I would routinely walk the beach in search of shells, agates, driftwood, rocks and other things to take with me to the studio. One day, there they were: grey, tall masses of wood pointing everywhere, built with pieces of driftwood or other debris that had washed ashore. I'd never seen the forts before in my life. Some of them held remnants of fires from the night before, where children sat and watched their parents dig for clams. Some fires were still burning.

They consumed me for the rest of my time at the residency. I searched miles and miles of beach for them.

Can you tell us a bit about your work surrounding driftwood forts?

There's this film, *The Subconscious Art of Graffiti Removal*, which takes a tongue-in-cheek look at graffiti removal. The film cleverly elevates the status of the people who paint over graffiti into high art. I thought, 'What if I could elevate driftwood sculptures in a similar way?' That's why I began documenting the materials used in the forts I found, as if I were writing an art book. But the project evolved into something different — social, too, with a website and an Instagram account. Pictures of forts have been sent in from Japan, New Zealand, Australia and the United States.

> "
> I'd never seen the forts before in my life. Some of them held remnants of fires from the night before, where children sat and watched their parents dig for clams. Some fires were still burning.

How did you first hear about the self-build culture?

In college I found out about the *Whole Earth Catalog*, which blew my mind. I was fascinated with the back-to-the-land movement, domes, yurts and the hippie lifestyle. I wanted to recreate that for myself.

What do you like about self-building?

I think starting from scratch, with limitless options, is possibly the most lifeless and boring way to build. My approach is to find something you love and make a plan based off of that. There's no way you're going to be bummed about what you make when you put all that intention and consideration into building around or incorporating that special thing.

How has your work in self-building evolved since you first started documenting driftwood forts?

I first started documenting forts and writing about the process in 2012. Later that year I moved to Los Angeles from Oregon to better establish myself in the art world. By 2014 I was living in a small duplex in the Lincoln Heights neighbourhood, tucked behind a larger house. I began to realise I needed a change. I often walked up the hill at the end of my street to a sort of no-man's-land, a series of mostly vacant lots with incredible views of the city. That was there I met Paige, who gave me the freedom and space to build a studio and convert an outbuilding on her property into a small house. It's a vast property, almost half a hectare (an acre): twenty or thirty fruit trees, doves in a giant walk-in aviary, chickens, quails, and now turkeys and a tortoise. It also has two non-adjoining structures, each about 18.5 square metres (200 square feet) in size. I saw the run-down state of the structures and how badly the trees needed care as the opportunity of a lifetime. I began building myself into the fabric of the place.

Are you trying to create a physical community around your self-build work in LA?

On my birthday, I hosted what was more or less a barn raising. Instead of having all my friends meet somewhere like a bar, we met at the site of what is now my studio and worked together to fix it up. I was initially shy about hosting something that would most definitely be benefitting me, but my friends assured me that the people helping would get something out of it, too – a shared sense of accomplishment. So we cleaned the site, put the roof on my studio, and ate and drank all day. I highly recommend this sort of activity, and I am hoping to host more of them for other friends. We can all help each other on the road to the next big thing.

How do you connect with nature in your day-to-day life?

Most days I'm tending to the trees or plants in some way. I feel more connected to nature here. The hillside is always buzzing with life, between the birds, squirrels and coyotes. I walk, run and hike throughout the week. I'm lucky to live where I do.

..........x

> "
> I saw the run-down state of the structures and how badly the trees needed care as the opportunity of a lifetime. I began building myself into the fabric of the place.

Acknowledgements

A huge thank you to our generous contributors whose heartfelt words and images make up this book and continually inspire us.

A special thanks to Padraig Croke, Elle Nikishkova, Ippei and Janine Naoi (Ippei & Janine Photography), and Nyree Jacobs for your outstanding contribution to this latest edition.

Thank you to the uber-talented Bec Kilpatrick for her wonderful illustrations, who, along with her partner Andrew Pavlidis, also provided some of the magnificent photography throughout the book.

Thank you to the skilled (and extremely patient!) team at Hardie Grant past and present – Melissa Kayser, Rosanna Dutson, Megan Cuthbert, Lauren Whybrow and Kate Armstrong.

Big thanks to Kåre Martens for his awesome design work, to Samuel Byrnes for the stunning cover design and to Megan Ellis for her masterful typesetting.

We would also like to thank our friends and family for encouraging us along the way. Thanks to Anais, Raffe and Theo – the Francis team is now complete, and we look forward to many adventures together.

Some of the material in this book originally appeared in *Homecamp*, published by Hardie Grant Travel, 2017, where full acknowledgements for individual contributions appear.

Published in 2021 by Hardie Grant Travel, a division of Hardie Grant Publishing

Hardie Grant Travel (Melbourne)
Wurundjeri Country
Building 1, 658 Church Street
Richmond, Victoria 3121

Hardie Grant Travel (Sydney)
Gadigal Country
Level 7, 45 Jones Street
Ultimo, NSW 2007

www.hardiegrant.com/au/travel

A catalogue record for this book is available from the National Library of Australia

Hardie Grant acknowledges the Traditional Owners of the Country on which we work, the Wurundjeri people of the Kulin Nation and the Gadigal people of the Eora Nation, and recognises their continuing connection to the land, waters and culture. We pay our respects to their Elders past, present and emerging.

Rewild
ISBN 9781741177596

10 9 8 7 6 5 4 3 2 1

Publisher
Melissa Kayser

Design
Kåre Martens

Senior editor
Megan Cuthbert

Cover design
Samuel Byrnes

Project editor
Rosanna Dutson

Typesetting
Megan Ellis

Colour reproduction by Megan Ellis and Splitting Image Colour Studio

Printed and bound in China by LEO Paper Products LTD.

The paper this book is printed on is certified against the Forest Stewardship Council® Standards and other sources. FSC® promotes environmentally responsible, socially beneficial and economically viable management of the world's forests.

Recipes disclaimer: All recipes use Australian measurements, such as 20 ml tablespoons and 250 ml cups.

Photography credits:
Front cover image: Ippei & Janine Photography
Back cover image: Brooke Holm
Endpapers: Padraig Croke (double pages and back single), Elle Nikishkova (front single)

All images shown within each story © the story's author, except for the following: ii–iii, 40–41, 76–77, 142–143, 176–177 Andrew Pavlidis; iv–v, xii, 15 Padraig Croke; vii, ix Hilary Walker; viii, x–xi, 22–23, 86–87 Brooke Holm; 28–29, 94–99, 178–179 Ippei & Janine Photography; 36, 38 Angus Kennedy; 75 Max Saeling/unsplash; 79 Rachel Kay Photography; 80–81, 84–85 Vic Phillips; 82 (top) Jonathan Cherry; 82 (bottom) Melissa Parsons; 144, 146 Shantanu Starick.

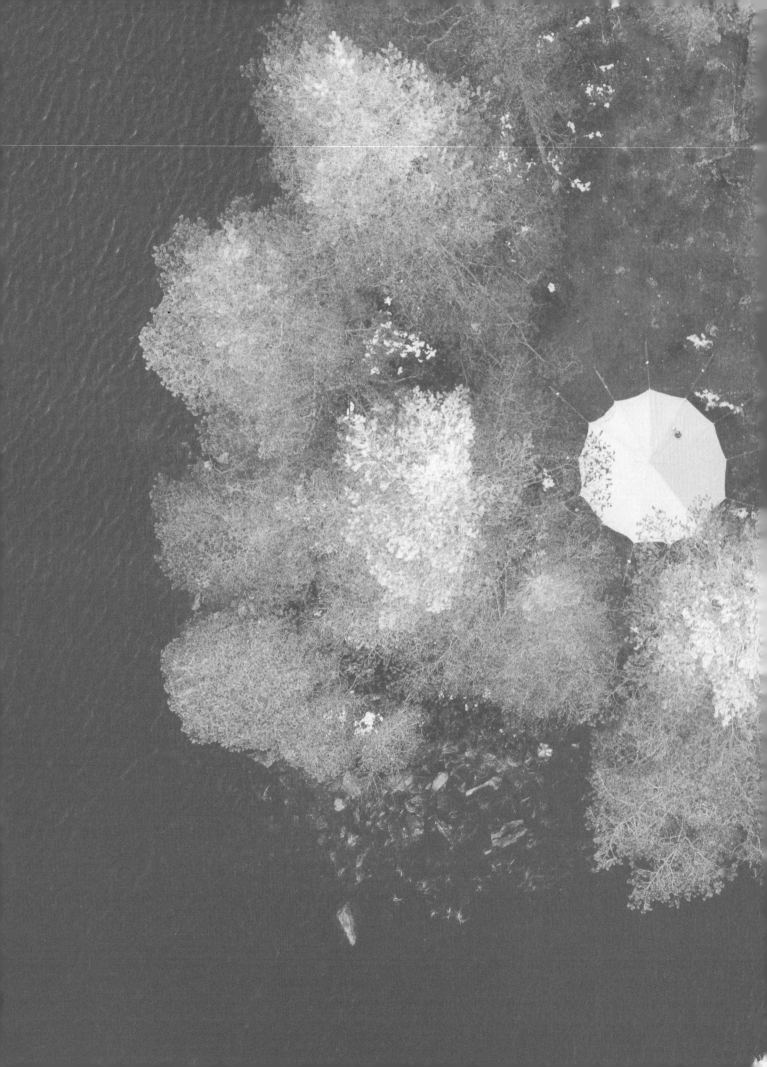